VEGAN
WITH A VENGEANCE

OVER 150 DELICIOUS CHEAP
ANIMAL-FREE
RECIPES

Isa Chandra Moskowitz

GRUB STREET • LONDON

Dedicated to my mom, Marlene Stewart, rn:

The most kick-ass nurse and mother NYC has ever known

This edition published in 2007 by

Grub Street
4 Rainham Close
London SW11 6SS
Email: food@grubstreet.co.uk
www.grubstreet.co.uk

Text copyright © Isa Chandra Moskowitz, 2007

Copyright this UK edition © Grub Street, 2007

Jacket and book designed by Lizzie Ballantyne

First published in the USA by Marlowe & Company

An imprint of Avalon Publishing Group Incorporated

The right of Isa Chandra Moskowitz to be identified as the author of this work has been asserted by her in accordance with the Copyright, Designs and Patents Act 1988

A CIP catalogue record for this book is available from the British Library

ISBN 1 904943 66 7 (10 digit)

ISBN 978-1-904943-66-2 (13 digit)

Printed and bound by MPG, Bodmin, Cornwall

CONTENTS

My first thank-you is for Justin; for typing, prepping, listening, going to the store, cleaning up after me, and ghostwriting the entire book for me while I lay in my hammock and fanned myself. Well, not quite, but still.

My testers—Jennifer Philburn, Adam Nelson, Jo Scovell, Drew Blood, Chris Poupart, Carrie Lynn Reilly, Paula Gross, Justin Walsh, Dominique Ryder, Kittee Berns, and Lynda Bartram. Not a day went by when I didn't check our testing site and think that you guys were awesome.

Terry Hope Romero, my partner in crime.

Denise Gaberman, Niharika Desai, and Lou Thomas for being part of *Post Punk Kitchen* and helping to make the most awesomest vegan cooking show in the world—without which there would be no cookbook.

Michelle Moskowitz Brown, for inspiring me and giving me honest feedback. Thanks to her hubby, Aaron, just because, and of course my nephew Maxwell Aaron Brown for being a beautiful baby. See Max? Tanta Isa put you in a book!

Erica Rose Levine, even though she didn't do anything she is my best friend and would kill me if I didn't thank her. Oh, she let me stay at her house and write so scratch that. And Amy Sims for proofreading things via Instant Messenger during the wee hours of the morning.

Michael Robert Cooper aka Mumbles for workshopping with me and being the wind beneath my wings (literally).

Marlowe & Company: Kylie Foxx for bearing with me through a computer meltdown and nervous breakdown, and Matthew Lore for accepting my proposal.

My literary agent—Marc Gerald at the Agency Group. Thanks for believing in me and realizing the potential my little idea had.

And lastly thanks to all the magazines and web sites that supported me and got the word out about *The Post Punk Kitchen*: Punk Planet, *Herbivore* magazine, *Satya* magazine, *Bust* magazine, *Venus* magazine, Nerdnyc.com, Vegblog.org, and Veganfreaks.org especially.

FOREWORD

by Ryan MacMichael, vegblog.org

I'm about as far removed from being "punk" as one can be. Or at least, I look that way. I'm more of a... how do you say?... a nerd. But one part of the punk aesthetic I've always connected with is the idea of "Do It Yourself." Whether it's in relation to music, publishing, or cooking, the unpolished, improvised nature of DIY projects results in something much more interesting than most overtly commercial efforts.

Vegetarians and vegans have long adopted the DIY philosophy because, let's face it, we don't live in a very vegan world. We have to be constantly creative, finding ways to adapt to situations that clearly don't have animals (or animal-friendly humans) in mind.

Never mind.

Vegan with a Vengeance has succeeded in not only bringing vegan cooking home, but bringing home cooking to vegans. Isa Chandra Moskowitz's recipes are both exotically creative and comfortingly accessible. Her avoidance of prepared convenience foods will help wean you from the corporate teat while at the same time saving you money and encouraging you to support local growers.

As you flip through the book you'll find that you come across recipes you've never seen before (BBQ Pomegranate Tofu) as well as fresh takes on old favourites (Scrambled Tofu). And this may be the first vegetarian cookbook ever that doesn't have a single salad recipe.

Isa has kindly laid out what you need in your kitchen to be a successful at-home vegan chef, both the equipment in your cupboards and the food in your pantry. If she can film a cooking show in her tiny Brooklyn kitchen, you'll be able to stock up on the bare essentials with no problems.

But the creativity doesn't end with the recipes. You'll get ideas about starting a brunch café, buying kitchen equipment without electrocuting yourself, and reading up on veganism on "teh Intarweb." Thanks to Isa's cat, Fizzle, I'm now well versed in food history. And I've accumulated enough "punk point" cooking tips that I'm hoping to cash them in for something more punk than my current work shirt.

Eating is a moral act or a political statement, depending on whom you ask. When you choose to stop eating animal products and supporting big business, you prove both statements to be correct. *Vegan with a Vengeance* will make that a lot easier. And it also helps me feel a little more punk.

INTRODUCTION

Welcome to *Vegan with a Vengeance* ! Here you'll find a collection of vegan recipes that I've created over the past sixteen years. Some recipes I dreamed up, some are classic favourites that I veganized, and some are dishes inspired by food that I've eaten at restaurants and just had to make for myself. Since the book says VEGAN in really big letters on the front cover and you probably wouldn't have picked it up if you weren't interested in vegan cooking, I am going to guess that you know all about veganism and think it's just great. So I am going to skip the song and dance about how healthy, ethical, and fun veganism can be.

I cook because I love to eat, it's as simple as that. But why *Vegan with a Vengeance*? It seems that many vegans depend on shop-bought processed food. Of course, I indulge in frozen veggie burgers now and then, but that's not the point. The point is that a vegan can go his or her whole life without ever laying a vegetable on a chopping board. I cringe at this notion for several reasons: (1) It is culinarily incorrect. Great cooks depend on fresh ingredients; nothing beats homemade. I am hell-bent on making a great cook out of each and every vegan. (2) It's expensive. One of the benefits of a vegan diet is its affordability. Beans bought in bulk will beat out a package of veggie sausage mix every time. (3) It makes us vegans dependent on huge corporations with shady policies. It's nicer to spend our money on locally grown vegetables and small independent businesses wherever possible. Don't worry, those veggie burgers will still be bought by people with heart problems or on diets, and I think that is more their target market anyway. OK, I've made my point— I promise that the heavy-handedness ends here.

···⟩ SO WHO AM I AND HOW DID I COME TO WRITE THIS COOKBOOK?

You deserve to know. After all, you are about to trust me with your taste buds. A cookbook isn't just light beach reading; it becomes a part of your life. In a few months' time it will be scribbled with your notes and splashed with tamari and tomato sauce.
Its food-stained, dog-eared pages will bring back memories of a potluck or the time you spilled an entire bottle of vanilla extract while baking your best friend's birthday cake.

My story begins in Brooklyn, New York. My mother swears that we were a family of domestics, baking cookies and wearing aprons, making light conversation over the chopping board. Passing the salt. I hate to disagree because she's my mother and I love her to pieces, but she taught me a lot of things and cooking wasn't one of them.

The fact was I spent most evenings eating dinner at friends' houses. No need to break out the violins; the cool thing about it was that growing up in Brooklyn and mooching off of everyone's parents gave me a wonderful sense of culinary diversity. Italian, Puerto Rican, Jewish, Indian—I got to experience it all and those tastes and flavours are a part of who I am and what I cook now.

The Brooklyn I grew up in wasn't the Brooklyn of today—that of lattes and Pilates, converted lofts and jogging strollers. It was more like "blast your underground disco, and throw McDonald's wrappers out your car window at anyone who dresses a little different or whom you suspect knows how to read." I was often confused and searching for real meaning—I knew that there was more to life then getting into fistfights with other big-haired girls in our local mall. So I started going to Manhattan with my best friend. And it wasn't the Manhattan of today—that of tenement-turned-luxury apartment and *Sex and the City* wannabes. It was exciting and artistic and "skateboarding is not a crime" and "Whose friggin park? Our friggin park!"

I had been hanging out more and more on the Lower East Side and getting involved with the anarchist scene there. I was not yet sure where my political affinities lay, but I knew that I respected what the activists and punks were doing: taking old decrepit buildings and turning them into homes, creating community gardens, making their own newspapers and magazines, and just generally giving a damn. I had already been listening to punk and dying my hair purple and making my own clothes. Vegetarianism was not a new concept to me—at the age of eight I made the horrifying connection that Puff Kit, our cat, was an animal just like the cows we ate. Once I started meeting people who were vegetarian it felt like the most logical and ethical way to be. I already knew that I didn't want to be part of a system of oppression; changing my diet was an easy and practical form of activism.

When I went vegetarian, food seemed to become the focal point of my life— volunteering for Food Not Bombs, cooking breakfast for everyone before a demonstration, making snacks as we silk-screened or made banners. I realized I had a knack for cooking and it was something that I enjoyed and everyone appreciated. I remember the first time I smelled basil fresh from the garden— I almost cried. I was hooked.

Flash forward to my thirties. After many culinary adventures—some of which you'll read about in this book—I wrote a cookbook, this cookbook in fact. It's quite the Cinderella story, except without all the sexism.

Not too long after September 11, which I had witnessed from my bedroom window, I was somewhat depressed and bored, feeling a bit like I was wasting my life. I was largely disconnected from the punk scene I grew up in; most of my old friends had drifted away. Dividing my time between an office job and cooking at a vegan café, I was also watching a lot of cooking shows on TV. This proved to be a volatile combination—I found myself doing my own cooking show in my head. I couldn't just prepare the BBQ tempeh and greens; I had to walk an imaginary audience through the whole thing.

It was while watching one particular TV chef butcher yet another innocent chicken that I thought, "Someone should really do a vegan cooking show." And then I realized, "I'm someone! I can do it!" If punk rock taught me anything, it's that we can create our own forms of entertainment. We don't have to sit back idly and wait for something to happen—we can make it happen. CRASS lyrics drifted through my head: "If the programme's not the one you want, get up and turn off the set. It's only you that can decide the life you're gonna get."

And so I took a month-long class at BCAT (Brooklyn Community Access TV) that taught me the basics of editing, camera work, and lighting. Then I spent weeks agonizing over what to call the show. I thought it had to be something that sounded vaguely punk because punk was the culture I grew up in and the culture that made me the woman I am. But I wasn't feeling that punk anymore—after all, I had a food processor and a job in an office. Fine—Post Punk. You know, not so punk anymore. The Post Punk Kitchen was born. At the time, I actually didn't realize that "post punk" was a thing unto itself—the music that came after punk—but, oh well, that's not what I meant. I meant it as sort of a self-conscious joke about the people with a punk rock ethos, like me, who are getting older and facing the conundrum of growing up and making compromises that their eighteen-year-old selves might hate them for.

I created a web site that instantly gained popularity by becoming a Yahoo! pick of the day. They wrote a very flattering review of my TV show. Thing was, I still didn't have a TV show. Shortly after that a magazine contacted me to do a little piece about the non-existent show. I was ecstatic. I called my friend and former vegan chef Terry and said, "Hey, want to be in this article with me?" She agreed. I then got her to agree to be the guest host in the first episode, which would feature sushi. Now, Terry is a complete sushi addict and she can't possibly say no to anything that shows off her sushi skills. (Little did she know that I was actually roping her into my cult and that she would never be able to escape.) Then my friend and upstairs neighbour, Denise, who worked in independent media and television production, said she was really excited about the idea of the show. She volunteered her collective production company to handle all the technical aspects.

When we actually started producing the show it seemed to strike a chord with people—two girls cooking in a real kitchen, making stupid sex jokes, and having a punk rock band in the living room chopping vegetables. I got so many wonderful letters over the following year—mothers with children that were lactose intolerant, seasoned vegans and vegetarians who wanted to thank us, people who just loved food and liked the show, new vegetarians with cooking questions. Lots of people asked if we had a cookbook, so I began to look into self-publishing.

Now comes the Cinderella part. Across the country, a big-shot Beverly Hills literary agent, dressed in white, smoking a Cuban cigar with pinky rings on his finger (that is my artistic embellishment; he's actually a mild-mannered Minor Threat fan originally from Ohio) called me and asked if he could pitch my book.

And now you're holding it in your hands. I hope that if you're a new cook, it will empower you to be fearless in the kitchen. I hope that if you are an experienced cook, you will enjoy my take on things. If only one dish is a success then my job here is done. But there better be a heck of a lot more than one.

I would love to hear from you. Check out The Post Punk Kitchen web site at **www.theppk.com**.

HOW TO USE THIS BOOK

Fizzle is my cat. He often sits on the worksurface while I prepare things. I know it's unsanitary, but really, there is no keeping him away, so I decided to put him to work in the book since he can't work in real life. (Fizzle doesn't actually know how to cook—he's just a cat.) Throughout the book he offers little tidbits of information that aren't necessarily integral to the recipe, but that you might want to know—like the fact that miso is thought to fight radiation sickness and that flax seeds contain omega-3 fatty acids.

You'll also see Punk Points throughout, little tips that help make cooking or preparing a dish easier, like my top-secret technique for preparing a butternut squash.

Other than that there is nothing mysterious going on—just follow the recipes and use my suggested substitutions if you need to. I remember once reading a cookbook that asked readers not to deviate from a recipe—well I say no such thing. Deviate all you want, recipes are mere guidelines and everyone has different tastes. If the final dish tastes good to you, then it's a success.

TOOLS AND KITCHEN STUFF

I have a love-hate relationship with kitchenware shops. On the one hand, I love looking at all the fancy cookware and appliances, but on the other hand, do I really need brightly enameled French saucepans? No. But of course I go ahead and buy one anyway. That's the problem. To help you avoid the same pitfalls, I've provided a list below of those items I actually use.

> A good knife is so totally necessary. It'll cost you about £50 new, but you only need one and it'll last a lifetime. I recommend a 20cm/8in chef's knife. Professional knife sharpeners are a dying breed, but if you can find one, have him/her sharpen your knife for you—those sharpeners they sell in stores are useless. Take care of your knife and it will take care of you!

> I know I said you only need one knife but a serrated knife is mighty handy, too— you can go cheap here, though. Not just for bread; you can cut tomatoes more easily with a serrated blade. Don't use it on onions, though, unless you need a really good cry.

> A paring knife is also useful. Not so much for paring, but for opening packages, cutting delicate things, etc. So you need three knives, really, a chef's knife, a serrated knife, and a paring knife. But that's it, for real this time.

> I used to have a wooden chopping board but the damned thing got wet and mildewy on me. Plus it was a pain to clean. Now I have one of those plastic chopping boards with a rubber grip bottom and it's great. It doesn't slide all over the place and I can just throw it in the sink and not worry about mould. Whatever you do, don't use a glass chopping board: they look cool but they'll just destroy your knives.

> Bowls for mixing. A set of stainless-steel bowls is a nice thing to have; you can drop them and they won't break. Plus they're cheap. I have a big heavy Pyrex bowl that I like to use for bread and hot things, but it's a pain to clean (it doesn't fit in the sink so well) and it's heavy. I also have little bowls and ramekins that I use but they're totally not necessary.

> A big cast iron frying pan will change your life. It adds great flavour plus iron to food and it gets hot and stays hot. New ones don't cost a lot and you can buy used ones, too—if there's rust on the pan, scrub it off with steel wool and then give the

pan a light coating of oil and place it in a hot oven to season it. Never ever wash your cast iron pans with soap, and don't scrub 'em too hard, either! After a while, cooking oil will coat the pans and bake on, giving them a non-stickish kind of surface that also protects the iron from rust. When this happens the pans will become easy to clean; just soak 'em for a few minutes in hot water and clean them with a brush. Then dry them; if they stay wet they'll rust.

> A nonstick frying pan is a good thing to have, too, one that won't dent easily and has
a solid, well-attached handle. Remember not to use metal utensils with a nonstick surface. If you scratch it, it'll start to flake off and then it's useless; you'll have to throw it out. So take care of it. Don't get it super-hot, either; use a cast iron frying pan for that sort of thing.

> A metal spatula (for the cast iron pan) and a wooden spatula (for the nonstick). I like those cheap metal spatulas with a thin, flexible paddle.

> Tongs are your best friend. I use them for flipping things and for grabbing things that are high up on shelves.

> It's nice to have smaller pans for smaller things. I use a nonstick pan for toasting spices and melting chocolate. Try to purchase one that you can put in the oven as well (with a handle that won't melt), which is great for frittatas.

> For years I had a charity shop 6.8 litre/12 pint pot that I used for everything, but some rice burned into it and it had a broken handle anyway, so I had to throw it out. Now I have a 4.5 litre/8 pint pot and a giant 11 litre/19 pint pot. I hardly ever use the giant pot but, when I need it, I really need it, so it's great to have.

> My sister gave me a cast iron griddle pan that she didn't want, and that thing has revolutionized my life. I don't know how I lived without it. And it's not a terribly expensive item, either, so I don't know why I didn't have one. So awesome.

> A big spoon for stirring things and a ladle for soups.

> A box grater for shredding things and a fine grater for shaving things, zesting lemons, etc.

> A nice peeler, preferably a Y-shaped serrated one for peeling veggies with thick skins.

> A whisk, for whisking!

> My rubber spatula melted when I left it too close to the stove. So I went and bought one of those silicon ones—problem solved. Great for getting all the batter out of the mixing bowls.

> A frying thermometer, not to be confused with a meat thermometer or a sugar thermometer. A frying thermometer can measure temperatures up to 260°C/475°F (the other thermometers quit at temperatures much lower than that), and should come with a clip or hook to let you hang the gizmo inside the pot.

> I buy baking sheets, muffin tins, etc., as I need them. A good baking tray is a must-have. Get a cheap 23 x 33cm/9 x 13in baking tin for roasting—stuff will burn and get stuck in it, so you don't want to use your good one. I really like my Pyrex casserole,
and my glass pie plate.

> I have a lot of baking accoutrements but the things I use every time I bake are my sieve and my wooden spoon.

> You don't want to do without a blender. It's great for whizzing tofu into a purée, or making pesto and other sauces. I use my blender almost daily.

⋯❖ **THINGS THAT I HAVE BUT THAT AREN'T TOTALLY NECESSARY**

> A handheld mixer for mixing batter.

> A handheld blender for puréeing soups.

> A small coffee grinder for grinding spices.

> A food processor for chopping, mixing dough, puréeing sauces, and making hummus. It may be too expensive to be essential, but if you get married or can find another way to register for gifts, someone might buy you one.

> A hammer or mallet for crushing seeds.

THE POST PUNK PANTRY

Nothing makes me happier than a well-stocked storecupboard. But of course I always find myself running out of cumin in the middle of cooking up a batch of scrambled tofu, or, halfway through mixing a cake I discover that I'm out of vanilla extract. So a well-stocked storecupboard is more of an ideal than a practical reality. Still, I've compiled this list of what my mythical well-stocked storecupboard would contain, as a guide for you.

⋯✣ HERBS, SPICES, AND SEASONINGS

> **Pre-ground Spices:** allspice, anise, black pepper in a pepper mill, cardamom, cayenne, chilli powder, Chinese five-spice, cinnamon, cloves, coriander, cumin, curry powder, ginger, nutmeg, paprika, turmeric.

> **Whole Spices:** cardamom seeds, cinnamon sticks, cloves, coriander seeds, cumin seeds, fennel seeds, mustard seeds, nutmeg.

> **Dried Herbs:** bay leaves, marjoram, oregano, rosemary, tarragon, thyme.

⋯✣ GRAINS AND RICE

> Arborio rice, basmati rice, brown rice, couscous (not technically a grain but still], millet, quinoa.

⋯✣ DRIED BEANS

> Black-eyed peas, black beans, chickpeas, Puy lentils, haricot beans, pinto beans, red lentils, split peas.

⋯✣ NUTS (stored in the freezer)

> Almonds, cashews, hazelnuts, macadamia nuts, peanuts, pumpkin seeds, walnuts.

⋯✣ CANNED GOODS

> Black beans, chickpeas, coconut milk, pineapple juice, tomato purée, whole tomatoes in juice.

PASTA AND NOODLES

> Linguine, macaroni, rice noodles, soba noodles.

BAKING STUFF

> Almond extract, arrowroot, plain flour, plain chocolate, baking powder, bicarbonate of soda, chocolate chips, cocoa powder, cornmeal, cornflour, flax seeds (whole or ground), lemon extract, maple extract, pure vanilla extract, raisins, rolled oats, desiccated coconut, tapioca starch (also called tapioca flour), wholemeal flour.

FROZEN FRUITS AND VEGGIES

> Artichoke hearts, sweetcorn, soy beans (edamame), peas, spinach, various berries and fruit.

IN THE FRIDGE

> Capers, Dijon mustard, extra-firm tofu, peanut butter, rice milk, soy milk, tahini, tempeh, vegannaise (vegan mayonnaise).

VINEGARS, OILS, AND LIQUID THINGS

> Cider vinegar, balsamic vinegar, brown rice syrup, rapeseed oil, olive oil, groundnut oil, pure maple syrup, red wine vinegar, rice wine vinegar, soy sauce, white cooking wine.

OTHER VEGAN MUST-HAVES:

> Nutritional yeast, textured vegetable protein, vital wheat gluten, extra-firm silken tofu (vacuum-packed).

BRUNCH

BRUNCH IS PROBABLY MY FAVOURITE MEAL
IN THE WORLD. I LOVE WAKING UP TO THE
SMELL OF ONIONS AND COFFEE AND
PANCAKES. IN REALITY IT'S USUALLY ME
DOING THE COOKING AND OTHERS WAKING
UP TO IT BECAUSE I'M GENEROUS LIKE THAT.
BUT FOR WHOEVER IS DOING THE COOKING,
TRY TO PREPARE AS MUCH AS YOU CAN THE
NIGHT BEFORE SO THAT YOU CAN ROLL OUT
OF BED AND GET THINGS GOING.

SCRAMBLED TOFU

SERVES 4

I eat scrambled tofu at least three times a week. This is my basic recipe but feel free to add any finely chopped vegetables that you want to use up; add them when you add the mushrooms. Broccoli, courgette, and cauliflower are all great contenders. The most important thing is that you get the texture right; you want it to be chunky. As you cook the tofu it will crumble more, so just break it into big chunks through your fingers right into the pan. This is a great tasting way to introduce a tofu-phobe to the heavenly bean curd we all know and love.

1 tablespoon olive oil
1 medium-size yellow onion, chopped into 1cm/1/2in chunks
150g/5oz thinly sliced cremini mushrooms
2 to 3 cloves garlic, finely chopped
450g/1lb extra-firm tofu, drained
4 tablespoons nutritional yeast
Juice of 1/2 lemon
1 carrot, peeled (optional, I grate it in at the end, mostly for colour)

For spice blend:
2 teaspoons ground cumin
1 teaspoon dried thyme, crushed with your fingers
1 teaspoon ground paprika
1/2 teaspoon ground turmeric
1 teaspoon salt

> Heat the oil in a frying pan over medium-high heat. Sauté the onions for 3 minutes, until softened; add the mushrooms, sauté for 5 minutes; add the garlic, sauté for 2 minutes. Add the spice blend and mix it up for 15 seconds or so. Add 50ml/2fl oz water to deglaze the pan, scraping the bottom to get all the garlic and spices.

> Crumble in the tofu and mix well. Don't crush the tofu, just kind of lift it and mix it around. You want it to remain chunky. Let cook for about 15 minutes, stirring occasionally and adding splashes of water if necessary to keep it from sticking too much. Lower the heat a bit if you find that the tofu is sticking. Add the lemon juice. Add the nutritional yeast and mix it up. If the mixture is sticking to the pan, add splashes of water. The moistness really depends on how much water the tofu was retaining before you added it.

> Grate the carrot into the tofu mixture and fold. Serve with guacamole and salsa and potatoes and toast and tempeh bacon.

> **Tofu Rancheros:** Add 225g/8oz salsa at the end, cook for 1 minute extra.

> **Asian-Style Scrambled Tofu:** Add 2 tablespoons of finely chopped ginger with the garlic, use groundnut oil instead of olive oil, substitute shiitake mushrooms, and omit the thyme and nutritional yeast. Mix in 75g/3oz thinly sliced spring onions at the very end.

‣ PUNK POINTS

> If you don't have nutritional yeast on hand you can still make this recipe; just don't add any water when cooking.

FIZZLE SAYS

Use a cast iron pan so that you don't have to worry about scratching the pan to get all the good burnt bits.

ASPARAGUS AND SUN-DRIED TOMATO FRITTATA

SERVES 4

A frittata is an open-faced, baked omelette. I love the combo of asparagus and sun-dried tomatoes for its colours as well as taste and texture, but you can get creative with your vegetable choices or use some of my variations below. No need to press the tofu, just drain it and give it a squeeze over the sink—that ought to do it.

450g/1lb extra-firm tofu
1 tablespoon soy sauce
1 teaspoon Dijon mustard (yellow will work fine if you like that better)
4 tablespoons nutritional yeast
2 teaspoons olive oil
1 small onion, cut into 5mm/1/4in dice
3 stalks asparagus, rough ends discarded, cut into bite-size pieces
275g/10oz sun-dried tomatoes packed in oil, finely chopped
2 cloves garlic, finely chopped
1 teaspoon dried thyme
4 teaspoons ground turmeric
Juice of 1/2 lemon
4 tablespoons fresh basil leaves, torn into pieces

> Preheat oven to 200°C/400°F/gas mark 6.

> In a mixing bowl, crumble the tofu and squeeze through your fingers until it resembles ricotta cheese. This should take about a minute. Mix in the soy sauce and mustard. Add the nutritional yeast and combine well. Set aside.

> In a small (20cm/8in) frying pan, sauté the onions in the olive oil for 2 minutes. Add asparagus and sun-dried tomatoes, sauté for about 3 more minutes. Add the garlic and thyme and turmeric, sauté for 1 more minute. Add the lemon juice to deglaze the pan; turn off the heat. Transfer the onion mixture to the tofu mixture and combine well. Fold in the basil leaves. Transfer back to the frying pan and press the mixture firmly in place. Cook in the oven at 200°C/400°F/gas mark 6 for 20 minutes. Transfer to the grill to brown the top, about 2 minutes (keep a close eye on it so as not to burn it). Let the frittata sit for 10 minutes before serving. Cut into four slices and lift each piece out with a pie server to prevent the frittata from falling apart. If it does crumble a bit, don't fret, just put it back into shape.

> **Broccoli and Olive Frittata:** Replace the asparagus with 50g/2oz chopped broccoli florets. Replace the sun-dried tomatoes with sliced black olives.

> **Indian Frittata:** Replace the asparagus with 50g/2oz chopped cauliflower florets. Replace the sun-dried tomatoes with 4 tablespoons cooked chickpeas. Omit the thyme and basil, add 1 teaspoon curry powder and one teaspoon cumin.

> **Mushroom Frittata:** Sauté 50g/2oz sliced cremini mushrooms along with the onions. Omit the asparagus, use 4 tablespoons sliced black olives or sun-dried tomatoes. Serve with Mushroom Sauce (page 91).

⋯⟐ **PUNK POINTS**

> If you don't have a 20cm/8in frying pan then use a pie plate when baking the fritatta.

START YOUR OWN BRUNCH CAFÉ

As a vegan, the hardest part about not eating eggs is going out with friends for brunch. That is one of the only times I feel resentment toward my omnivore associates: when I am sitting in a café as they enjoy waffles and omelettes and I have to make do with a bowl of porridge. But you can take the matter into your own hands and start your own brunch café—it's more fun and more social than having a hungover waiter spill coffee on you.

First, you need to decide on a space. When I lived in a loft this was easy—we had a huge open space available to us and we were able to pack the place with as many as fifty people on any given Sunday. But if you have a smaller space to work with, clear everything out of the biggest room, throw some pillows on the floor, or get a huge communal table. I've hosted cafés at bookstores and even in a church basement.

For the food, the easiest thing to do is prepare dishes that are easy to cook in large quantities and keep warm. Here is my typical menu:

⋯⟩ BREAKFAST BURRITOS

Cook a huge batch of scrambled tofu. Keep it warm on the top of the cooker over very low heat, stirring whenever you get a chance. Prepare a lot of guacamole and fresh salsa. Shred a few blocks of soy cheese beforehand (totally optional, the burritos are just as good without it). Buy flour tortillas and roll the tofu and cheese into a burrito, with a dollop of guac and salsa on top.

⋯⟩ HERB-ROASTED POTATOES (PAGE 33)

These keep well all day, either in a 110°C/225°F/gas mark 1/4 oven or in a portable heated serving tray. Serve with the breakfast burritos.

⋯✧ TEMPEH BACON (PAGE 31)

Keep warm in a portable heated serving tray or in a 110°C/225°F/gas mark 1/4 oven.

⋯✧ WAFFLES

Make all the waffles the night before and refrigerate. You'll just need to reheat them in a toaster the next day; sometimes they taste even better than fresh waffles because they get crispier when they are toasted. Serve with sliced strawberries and bananas and maple syrup.

⋯✧ TOFU, POTATOES, AND TEMPEH

Make another dish out of the scrambled tofu with roasted potatoes and tempeh, serve with a tortilla or toast.

Have a huge pot of coffee freshly brewed at all times. You can use a flask for the coffee and set up a coffee-serving station with the sugar and soy milk so guests can fix their own.

When I used to throw brunch cafés, we'd usually charge around £2.50 per person, which always covered costs and even netted some cash to invest in the next café. The point obviously isn't to make money, but to have a good time. We sometimes got a DJ to spin hip-hop, punk, and '80s music, so it was really more of a party during the day. I definitely suggest playing some music, whatever you like, and if you have some board games and cards, they'll make things even more (nerdy) fun.

TEMPEH AND WHITE BEAN SAUSAGE PATTIES

MAKES 10 PATTIES

I love the combination of white beans and tempeh. The beans have a naturally smoky flavour, and the tempeh and herbs give these patties the savoury taste I crave upon rolling out of bed on a Sunday morning or (let's be honest) afternoon. They have a softer texture than shop-bought vegetarian sausage patties, but a much better flavour. You can prepare the mix up to two days in advance so that all you have to do the day of serving is form the patties and cook.

450g/1lb tempeh, crumbled into bite-size pieces
4 teaspoons tamari (or soy sauce for that matter)
150g/5oz cooked white beans
3 tablespoons olive oil
2 cloves garlic, finely chopped
1 teaspoon fennel seeds, crushed
1 heaped tablespoon chopped fresh thyme
1 heaped teaspoon chopped fresh sage, (about 5 leaves)
Pinch of ground cayenne pepper
Pinch of ground nutmeg
1 tablespoon tomato purée
4 tablespoons plain bread crumbs
Dash of salt
A few dashes fresh black pepper

> Place the tempeh into a saucepan and just barely cover with water (it's OK, even preferable, if some of the tempeh is peeking out of the water). Add 1 teaspoon of tamari, cover and bring to a boil. Simmer for about 15 minutes, or until most of the water is absorbed. Drain any remaining water and transfer the tempeh to a large bowl. Add the white beans, give a quick stir, and set aside. This will heat the beans just a bit for easier mashing and cool the tempeh down just a bit for easier handling.

> Give the saucepan a quick rinse and dry. Sauté the garlic and fennel seed in 1 tablespoon olive oil over low heat, just until fragrant (about 1 minute). Add the remainder of the spices and stir constantly for 30 seconds. Add to the tempeh mixture along with the tomato purée and remaining tamari.

> Mash everything together with a potato masher or strong fork, until it's just a bit chunky and there are no whole beans left (you don't want it puréed, you should still be able to see the beans). Add the bread crumbs and combine well with a fork. Taste for salt and spices and adjust to your liking. Let sit for about 15 minutes to allow the flavours to meld.

> Form into patties, using about 3 tablespoons of the mix per pattie. Heat the remaining 2 tablespoons of olive oil over medium heat. Cook the patties until brown, about 3 minutes each side. You may need to add a little more oil when you flip them over.

SERVES 4 TO 6 AS A SIDE DISH

I often enjoy this delicious dish with a breakfast burrito; however, it makes a great accompaniment to any meal with Latin flair. Ancho chilli powder tastes best here but if you can't find it and don't feel like making your own, you can substitute regular chilli powder.

2 tablespoons olive oil
1 medium-size onion, very finely chopped
3 cloves garlic, finely chopped
1 teaspoon salt
2 teaspoons coriander seeds, crushed
2 teaspoons cumin seeds, crushed
1/2 teaspoon fennel seeds, crushed
2 tablespoons ancho chilli powder
1 teaspoon dried oregano
1 tablespoon sugar
750ml/1 1/4 pints water
150g/5oz Textured Vegetable Protein (TVP)
2 bay leaves
1 cinnamon stick
3 tablespoons tomato purée
A very healthy dose freshly ground black pepper

> Preheat a medium-size saucepan for a minute or so, add the oil and onion and sauté for 3 minutes. Add the garlic and sauté for another 30 seconds; add the salt, spices, and sugar; sauté for another 2 minutes. Add the water, TVP, bay leaves, cinnamon stick, and tomato purée, cover and bring to a boil. Lower heat and simmer for 10 more minutes. Uncover and remove the cinnamon stick; cook for 5 minutes more, uncovered, until most of the water has been absorbed and reduced. Add freshly ground pepper to taste. You can serve immediately but I prefer to cover and let sit for 20 or so minutes to let the TVP absorb all the flavours.

⋯﹖ PUNK POINTS

To crush the seeds quickly, place them in a coffee grinder and pulse three or four times. If you are too punk for a coffee grinder, place the seeds in a plastic bag and cover with a thin towel or even a few pieces of newspaper, and proceed to hammer with a mallet or a regular hammer, until the neighbours complain.

FIZZLE SAYS

Textured Vegetable Protein, often called TVP, is soy beans that have been defatted, pressure cooked, and dried, leaving only the protein. The end product is sold in small dry chunks at health food shops. Once rehydrated and cooked, TVP has a chewy, meaty texture. It comes in small or large chunks. We prefer to use the small chunks but the large ones will work as well.

TEMPEH SAUSAGE CRUMBLES

SERVES 4

When I first began writing this book I wasn't sure what section to put this recipe into because I use it in so many different kinds of meals—in pasta sauce, in gravy, as a side dish for brunch. I decided to put it here, but don't be afraid to experiment with it.

225g/8oz tempeh
1 tablespoon fennel seeds
1 teaspoon dried basil
1 teaspoon dried marjoram or oregano
1/2 teaspoon red chilli flakes
1/2 teaspoon dried sage
2 cloves garlic, finely chopped
2 tablespoons tamari or soy sauce
1 tablespoon olive oil
Juice of 1/2 lemon

> In a small pan, crumble the tempeh and add enough water to almost cover it. Over medium-high heat, simmer the tempeh until most of the water is absorbed, about 12–15 minutes or until the water is mostly absorbed. Drain the remaining water and add the rest of the ingredients and cook over medium heat, stirring occasionally, until lightly browned, about 10 minutes.

MAKES 12 OR SO STRIPS

I love these smoky strips alongside pancakes, or in a BLT or in a salad or in a house or with a mouse. They aren't going to fool any meat eaters, but they'll fully satisfy us herbivores. You need to marinade the tempeh for a good hour so plan ahead or marinate it overnight. Groundnut oil adds a richer flavour so I recommend using it, but rapeseed or vegetable oil will do nicely. You can use thinly sliced, pressed tofu if you haven't got any tempeh.

3 tablespoons tamari or soy sauce
5 tablepoons cider
1 teaspoon tomato purée
1/4 teaspoon liquid smoke
225g/8oz tempeh
2 cloves garlic, crushed
2 tablespoons groundnut oil or vegetable oil

> To make the marinade, combine the tamari, cider, tomato purée, and liquid smoke in a wide, shallow bowl and mix with a fork until the tomato purée is fully dissolved. Set aside.

> Cut the tempeh into thin strips (less than 5mm/1/4in thick) lengthwise. You should be able to get about twelve strips. Rub the strips with the crushed garlic, then toss the garlic cloves into the marinade. Submerge the tempeh strips in the marinade and let sit, turning occasionally, for at least an hour and up to overnight. After marinating, discard the garlic.

> Heat the groundnut oil in a large frying pan over medium heat. Add the tempeh strips and cook for 4 minutes on one side; the bottom should be nicely browned. Flip the strips over and pour the remainder of the marinade over them; if there isn't much marinade left add a splash of water. Cover and let cook for 3 more minutes, until the liquid is absorbed. Uncover and check for doneness; if necessary, keep cooking uncovered until all sides are nicely browned. Remove from heat and serve.

TEMPEH BACON

SWEET POTATO HASH WITH FIVE-SPICE AND WATERCRESS

SERVES 6

I whipped this up one morning to go with my scrambled tofu when the only vegetables I had around were sweet potatoes and watercress. The watercress made me think Chinese, and the Chinese made me think five-spice powder and thus this simple but delicious creation was born. The watercress does a great job of picking up the spices and the garlic.

3 tablespoons olive oil
1 medium-size onion, cut into 5mm/$1/4$in dice
2 cloves garlic, finely chopped
$1/4$ teaspoon salt
$11/2$ teaspoons Chinese five-spice powder
3 medium-size sweet potatoes, cut into 1cm/$1/2$in dice
1 bunch watercress, stems discarded, torn into big pieces

> In a large frying pan over medium-high heat, cook the onion in 1 tablespoon of the olive oil for 2 minutes, stirring occasionally. Add the garlic, salt, and five-spice and cook for about 1 minute. Add the sweet potatoes and the rest of the oil. Cook for about 12 to 15 minutes, until the potatoes are cooked and caramelized a bit. Add the watercress and cook, stirring constantly, for 2 more minutes.

FIZZLE SAYS

Chinese five-spice powder incorporates the five basic tastes of Chinese cooking—sweet, sour, bitter, pungent and salty. The blend commonly sold consists of cinnamon, black pepper, cloves, fennel seed, and star anise.

SERVES 4–6

You can't have brunch without potatoes—I'd like to see you try. I love these crispy, salty spuds and they are all kinds of easy to prepare. If the small red potatoes are radically different sizes, then cut the larger ones into thirds. They should be approximately 3cm/1¼in across.

1.3kg/3lb small red potatoes, halved widthwise
1 medium-size onion, quartered and sliced 1cm/½in thick
3 tablespoons olive oil
2 teaspoons coarse sea salt
Several dashes fresh black pepper
4 teaspoons rosemary, chopped
4 teaspoons chopped fresh thyme

> Preheat oven to 230°C/450°F/gas mark 8. Divide the potatoes and onions between two rimmed baking tins or a large baking tray, sprinkle with oil and then salt and pepper, and toss to coat (I find it's easiest to use your hands for this). Roast for 35 minutes. Remove from oven, sprinkle with the herbs, toss to coat (use a spatula now, they're hot! I'm sure you realize this but just in case...). Return to oven and roast until brown and tender, about 20 minutes longer.

HERB-ROASTED POTATOES

MAKES 12–14 BISCUITS

This biscuit recipe is adapted from a 1944 cookbook entitled *Ruth Wakefield's Toll House Tried and True Recipes*. In her introduction she states, "I know there are no substitutions for butter, cream, eggs, fresh fruits and vegetables for preparing a fine meal." I agree with the fruit and veggies part but aside from that I have thoroughly ignored Ruth's advice, and her modified biscuit recipe has served me well for years. If you'd like, you can serve these with the White Bean Sausage Gravy (recipe follows), the Mushroom Sauce on page 91 or ignore my suggestions as I did Ruth's and serve them with margarine or whatever else you want. The gravy is a modified version of a recipe submitted to my web site by someone named Lisa. Thanks, Lisa.

225g/8oz plain flour
5 teaspoons baking powder
1 teaspoon salt
3 tablespoons non-hydrogenated shortening
3 tablespoons non-hydrogenated margarine
150ml/¹/₄ pint rice or soy milk

> Preheat oven to 230°C/450°F/gas mark 8. Lightly grease a baking sheet.

> Sift together the flour, baking powder, and salt. Cut the shortening and margarine into the flour with a pastry knife or your fingers. Add the rice milk to form a soft dough. Mix well and pat out on a floured worksurface until about 1cm/¹/₂in thick; cut out 5cm/2in rounds with the rim of a glass or biscuit cutter. Place on prepared baking sheet and bake for 12 to 15 minutes.

WHITE BEAN AND TEMPEH SAUSAGE GRAVY

MAKES ENOUGH TO COVER 12–14 BISCUITS

Tempeh Sausage Crumbles (page 30)
275g/10oz cooked white beans or 400g/14oz can white beans,
  drained and rinsed
2 tablespoons olive oil or margarine, softened
3 tablespoons vegetable stock or water
1/2 teaspoon salt
A few dashes fresh black pepper
10 to 12 leaves fresh sage, chopped

> Prepare the Tempeh Sausage Crumbles and keep them warm in the pan.

> Purée the white beans with the olive oil and vegetable stock in a blender or food processor until relatively smooth. Add to the tempeh crumbles along with the salt and pepper. Heat through for a few minutes. If you want to make the gravy thinner, add a little more vegetable stock. Mix in the sage and cook for another 2 minutes.

"FRONCH" TOAST

MAKES 12–15 SLICES

I couldn't tell you what it is about chickpea flour but this French toast looks and tastes just like the "real" thing. Chickpea flour is quite easy to find these days—if you don't have a Middle Eastern food shop nearby, try a health food shop or your local deli. I like to use a nice crusty baguette for this recipe, but if you want to use sliced bread, make sure to lightly toast it first (see below). Serve with fresh berries, sliced bananas, and pure maple syrup.

Loaf of Italian or French bread, baguette shaped, preferably stale
120ml/4fl oz soy cream
   (rice or soy milk would make a good substitution, preferably rice)
120ml/4fl oz rice milk or plain soy milk
2 tablespoons cornflour
4 tablespoons chickpea flour
Several tablespoons rapeseed or vegetable oil

> Slice the bread into 2.5cm/1in rounds. The bread should be a bit stale; if not, leave the slices out overnight or put them in a 180°C/350°F/gas mark 4 oven for 3 to 4 minutes to dry them out—you don't want to toast them. (If you're in a rush, feel free to skip this step—the French toast will still taste good.)

> Pour the soy cream and rice milk into a wide, shallow bowl. Mix in the cornflour and stir until dissolved. Add the chickpea flour and mix until it is mostly absorbed; some lumps are OK.

> Heat a nonstick frying pan over medium-high heat. Add enough oil to create a thin layer on the bottom (a tablespoon or two).

> Soak the bread slices (as many as will fit into your pan) in the mixture and transfer to the frying pan. Cook each side for about 2 minutes; if they are not brown enough when you flip them, heat for 1 or 2 more minutes on each side. They should be golden brown with flecks of dark brown. Serve immediately.

PERFECT PANCAKES

There is nothing like a stack of pancakes dripping with maple syrup, served with some smoky tempeh bacon on the side. Although pancake ingredients are fairly simple, the combination of flour and water seems to have an uncanny ability to stress a person out. I'm no motivational speaker, but trust me—it may take a couple of tries to get perfect pancakes but you can do it. Here are some tips to guide you along the way. (If it helps, picture my head in a dream cloud floating above your left shoulder, guiding you on. If that doesn't help and only serves to freak you out, then just follow these guidelines.)

> The amount of water you need depends on several factors including altitude and the humidity in the air on any given day. I suggest using the liquid quantities I give as a guideline. First, add 250ml/8fl oz of water. If the batter looks too thick, or if your first pancake doesn't bubble up, add the remaining liquid.

> Don't overmix the batter. You want a couple of lumps in the flour; overmixed batter results in rubbery pancakes.

> You may notice that pancakes get lighter and fluffier as you get to the end of the batter. That's because the gluten in the flour has had some time to relax. Let your pancake batter sit for 10 minutes or so before proceeding. You can even let it sit overnight, covered and refrigerated. If the batter thickens too much, just add a little water to reconstitute it.

> Use a heavy-bottomed nonstick frying pan for even cooking. Or, you can use a cast iron pan because it's naturally nonstick.

> Make sure the pan is hot enough, but not smoking. Preheat the pan for 2 minutes and that should do the trick. If you flick a couple of drops of water into the pan, the drops should bounce. You can also do a test with a tablespoon or two of batter.

> Don't go crazy with the grease. A very thin coating of oil will do it. Use a spray bottle of rapeseed oil for an even coating. Apply a fresh coat every time you start a new batch.

> To form your pancakes into perfect circles, use the same amount of batter in a ladle every time. Pour the batter out with a slightly circular motion so that it spreads evenly. Don't just plop it down or the middle will be thicker than the edges. You can also try using a meat baster; just fill it up and squeeze the pancake batter out. You'll be amazed at the perfect circles this creates.

> The most important thing is that you don't give up. Some say the first pancake is always a flop, so just keep trying. You will get the hang of it!

PANCAKES

Straight up pancakes — simply great drizzled with maple syrup

150g/5oz plain flour
2 teaspoons baking powder
1/2 teaspoon salt
1 teaspoon ground cinnamon (optional)
2 tablespoons rapeseed oil (any mild tasting vegetable oil will do)
    plus oil for the pan
5 tablespoons water
300ml/1/2 pint plain rice or soy milk
1 teaspoon vanilla extract
2 tablespoons pure maple syrup

> Oil a large frying pan and preheat over medium-high heat about 2 minutes (see Perfect Pancakes page 37).

> Sift together the flour, baking powder, and salt, and cinnamon, if using. In a separate bowl, combine all the other ingredients. Adding wet ingredients to dry, mix until just combined. Do not overmix or the pancakes will be tough; a couple of lumps are OK.

> Cook pancakes until browned on the bottom and bubbles form on top, about 4 minutes. Turn the pancakes over and cook until the bottoms are browned and the pancakes are barely firm to touch. Transfer to individual plates. Repeat with remaining batter, adding more oil to the pan as needed.

···> VARIATIONS

> **Raspberry Lime:** Fold in 115g/4oz of fresh raspberries and 1 tablespoon of finely grated lime zest.

> **Blueberry:** Fold in 115g/4oz of fresh blueberries.

MAKES ABOUT SIX 15-18CM/6-7IN PANCAKES OR TEN 10CM/4IN ONES

Coconut and nutmeg are a great combination. To transform your kitchen into a tropical paradise, serve these pancakes with pineapple sauce (recipe follows) which is ridiculously easy to make.

150g/5oz plain flour
2 teaspoons baking powder
1/2 teaspoon salt
1 teaspoon ground or freshly grated nutmeg
  (if using fresh, it's one-third of a whole nutmeg)
5 tablespoons water
300ml/1/2 pint plain rice or soy milk
2 tablespoons pure maple syrup
1 teaspoon vanilla extract, or use coconut extract if you have it on hand
2 tablespoons rapeseed oil (any mild tasting vegetable oil will do),
  plus oil for the pan
75g/3oz desiccated coconut

> Oil a large frying pan and preheat over medium-high heat about 2 minutes (see Perfect Pancakes page 37).

> Sift together the flour, baking powder, salt, and nutmeg. Create a well in the centre of the dry ingredients; add the water, rice milk, maple syrup, vanilla, and oil. Mix until just combined, fold in coconut.

> If making large pancakes, use a ladle to pour the batter into the pan; most standard ladles will yield a 15cm/6in pancake. For smaller pancakes, drop 3 tablespoons batter into the pan. Cook until bubbles form on top, about 3 minutes. Turn pancakes over and cook until the bottoms are browned and the pancakes are cooked through, about 2 more minutes. Serve immediately or keep warm on a plate covered with foil while you cook the others. Repeat with remaining batter. Serve with pineapple sauce.

PINEAPPLE SAUCE

MAKES 475ML/16FL OZ

500g/11/4lb can pineapple chunks in juice
2 tablespoons arrowroot powder
3 tablespoons sugar
1 teaspoon vanilla extract

> In a saucepan, off the heat, stir the pineapple and juice with the arrowroot until it is dissolved; stir in sugar and vanilla. Over medium heat, stir often until the sauce thickens (about 7 minutes).

BANANA-PECAN PANCAKES

MAKES 9 SMALL PANCAKES

I called these Banana-Pecan Pancakes just to get your attention; the truth is you can use any nut you like, or even chocolate chips instead. Banana provides great flavour, and of course also makes for a wonderful, fluffy pancake. I made a vow not to use the word "crowd-pleaser" in this cookbook but I am going to sell out and tell you—these are a great crowd-pleaser! Everyone loves them. These cook up thicker than the other pancake recipes so I recommend making smaller pancakes and cooking them three to a pan.

175g/6oz plain flour
1 1/2 teaspoons baking powder
1/2 teaspoon bicarbonate of soda
1/4 teaspoon salt
1/8 teaspoon ground cinnamon
4 medium bananas, very well-mashed
350ml/12fl oz soy milk plus 1 teaspoon vinegar (let sit for 5 minutes)
1 tablespoon rapeseed oil
1 teaspoon vanilla extract
50g/2oz pecans, chopped
Rapeseed oil or cooking spray for the pan

> Sift together the flour, baking powder, bicarbonate of soda, salt, and cinnamon.

> In a separate bowl, mix the mashed banana with the soy milk, oil, and vanilla until pretty smooth. Pour the wet ingredients into the dry and mix but do not overmix. Fold in the pecans.

> Brush a large nonstick frying pan with rapeseed oil or spray with cooking spray and heat over medium-high heat until hot but not smoking. Working in batches of three, pour 3 tablespoons of batter per pancake into the hot frying pan and cook until bubbles appear on the surface and the undersides are golden brown, 1 to 2 minutes. Flip the pancakes with a spatula and cook until golden brown and cooked through, 1 to 2 minutes more. Transfer to a large plate and loosely cover with foil to keep warm, then make more pancakes, brushing or spraying the frying pan with oil for each batch.

> Serve with sliced bananas and maple syrup.

MAKES ABOUT SIX 15-18CM/6-7IN PANCAKES OR TEN 10CM/4IN ONES

I know. Chocolate for breakfast. Reserve this one for special occasions like Valentine's Day, or don't, just go ahead and be decadent. Serve with Strawberry Sauce (page 234) or fresh raspberries and maple syrup.

130g/4$1/2$oz plain flour
3 tablespoons cocoa powder
2 teaspoons baking powder
$1/2$ teaspoon salt
5 tablespoons water
300ml/$1/2$ pint rice or soy milk
2 tablespoons rapeseed oil
3 tablespoons pure maple syrup
1 teaspoon vanilla extract
$1/2$ teaspoon almond extract (optional)
50g/2oz plain chocolate chips
Rapeseed oil or cooking spray for pan

> In a large mixing bowl sift together the flour, cocoa powder, baking powder, and salt. Create a well in the centre of the flour mixture and add the water, rice milk, oil, maple syrup, and extracts. Mix until just combined, fold in chocolate chips.

> Oil and preheat a large frying pan over medium-high heat for about 2 minutes.

> If making large pancakes, use a ladle to pour the batter into the pan; most standard ladles will yield a 15cm/6in pancake. For smaller pancakes, drop 3 tablespoons batter into the pan. Cook until bubbles form on top, about 3 minutes. Turn pancakes over and cook until bottoms are browned and the pancakes are cooked through, about 2 more minutes. Serve immediately or keep warm on a plate covered with foil while you cook the others. Repeat with remaining batter.

CHOCOLATE-CHOCOLATE CHIP PANCAKES

WAKING UP TO MOM

I wouldn't call my mother a saint, but she certainly put up with quite a bit during my adolescence. When my sister and I reached our mid-teens we took to hanging out on the Lower East Side (LES) rather than on Sheepshead Bay, where we lived, because we grew tired of the comments and stuff people threw at us from their car windows.

The LES was a safe place, where we could wander the streets 'til the sun came up. We met people from all over who had travelled to New York to fight in the revolution of the time—fixing up and building the squats, keeping the police at bay, and trying to lay claim to a place of their own. Sometimes we brought the LES back with us to Sheepshead Bay, either because there was a demonstration coming up and we needed to paint banners in the basement or because we managed to bring the punks out to Brighton Beach for a late night party and dip in the water.

In the morning, my mom would awake to a dozen or so strange people scattered about, some in the living room, some making breakfast in the kitchen. "Mom," I would say, "This is Larry, this is Vegan Mike, this is Happy Mike, this is Dirtbag Mike." She'd politely smile and then ask to see me in her room, where she'd promptly slam the door and yell:

"Dirtbag Mike! I have to wake up to Dirtbag Mike?!" (While she had closed the door for privacy, you know the punks were cringing as her voice ripped through the house.)

"Well, yes, but there's also Happy Mike." (Did she have a problem looking at the bright side?)

Expletives would follow. Scrambled tofu was left to burn as my mom geared into the business of throwing everyone out. Usually not everyone left. The wise ones knew that if they waited out the storm, the sun would come out and my mom would either cook us all tofu balls and spaghetti or order cheeseless pizza for the brave stragglers who remained. Such was life in Sheepshead Bay in the late '80s. We didn't know at the time that we were ushering in a new age when our lip rings would become not only fashionable but, eventually, passé. It was simultaneously gratifying and horrifying to go back to the old neighbourhood in the '90s and see those same guys who once threw a McDonald's Shake at me years ago now sporting blue Mohawks. I suppose I could truly measure progress if now they threw a block of tofu at me instead. I'm still waiting.

MAKES 12 REGULAR WAFFLES OR 4–6 BELGIAN WAFFLES

When grating the pear for these waffles, leave the skin on—it adds a nice texture and interesting flecks of colour. It's best if you choose a pear that is a little under-ripe, which makes the grating easier and gives off less moisture. If you want to add even more gingery goodness, fold in a tablespoon of finely chopped crystallized ginger.

225g/8oz plain flour
2 teaspoons baking powder
1 teaspoon bicarbonate of soda
$1/2$ teaspoon salt
2 teaspoons ground ginger
$1/2$ teaspoon ground cinnamon
$1/4$ teaspoon ground allspice
$1/4$ teaspoon ground or freshly grated nutmeg
250ml/8fl oz pear or apple juice
175ml/6fl oz soy milk
5 tablespoons apple sauce
2 tablespoons corn oil (rapeseed or vegetable oil will do)
4 tablespoons sugar
2 teaspoons vanilla extract
1 pear, grated

> Preheat waffle iron according to the manufacturer's directions.

> Sift together the flour, baking powder, bicarbonate of soda, salt, and spices in a large mixing bowl. In a medium-size bowl, mix together the juice, soy milk, apple sauce, oil, sugar, and vanilla until well combined. Create a well in the centre of the flour mixture and slowly blend the wet ingredients into the dry until combined. Fold in the grated pear.

> Make your waffles according to the manufacturer's directions. I use a Belgian waffle iron, and 250ml/8fl oz batter per waffle works for me. For crispier waffles, let cook 30 seconds to a minute longer than the directions suggest.

GINGER-PEAR WAFFLES

OATMEAL-BANANA-RAISIN WAFFLES

MAKES 12 REGULAR WAFFLES OR 4–6 BELGIAN WAFFLES

I love the texture the oatmeal gives these waffles. They are chewy and have a hint of banana and cinnamon, with sweet bursts of raisins.

130g/4¹/₂oz plain flour
2 teaspoons baking powder
1 teaspoon bicarbonate of soda
1¹/₄ teaspoons ground cinnamon
¹/₄ teaspoon ground nutmeg
¹/₂ teaspoon salt
90g/3¹/₂oz rolled oats
1 very ripe medium-size banana
350ml/12fl oz soy milk
3 tablespoons pure maple syrup
3 tablespoons vegetable oil
115g/4oz raisins
Extra sliced bananas for the top

> Preheat waffle iron according to the manufacturer's directions.

> In a mixing bowl sift together the flour, baking powder, bicarbonate of soda, cinnamon, nutmeg, and salt. Add the oats and toss together.

> In a separate bowl mash the banana very well. Add the soy milk, maple syrup, and vegetable oil. I use a handheld blender to blend everything together; if you don't have one mix vigorously with a strong fork until there are very few clumps of banana left. Add the wet ingredients to the dry and mix just until combined. Fold in the raisins. Let the batter sit for 2 minutes before making the waffles; this allows the oats to get moist and blend with the rest of the batter.

> Prepare the waffles according to the manufacturer's directions. Serve with margarine, maple syrup, and sliced bananas on top.

Lemon + corn = heaven. Lemon + corn + blueberries = the VIP section of heaven. You can even up the ante by drizzling a little Macadamia Crème (page 235) over the Blueberry Sauce (recipe follows).

165g/5^1/$_2$oz plain flour
2 teaspoons baking powder
1 teaspoon bicarbonate of soda
^{1}/$_2$ teaspoon salt
75g/3oz cornmeal
3 tablespoons corn oil (vegetable or rapeseed oil will do)
475ml/16fl oz soy milk
4 tablespoons soy yogurt
Zest and juice from 2 lemons
4 tablespoons sugar

> Preheat waffle iron according to the manufacturer's directions.

> Sift together the flour, baking powder, bicarbonate of soda, salt, and cornmeal in a large mixing bowl. In a medium-size bowl, mix together the oil, soy milk, soy yogurt, lemon juice, and sugar until well combined. Create a well in the centre of the flour mixture and mix in the wet ingredients just until combined. Make your waffles according to the manufacturer's directions.

BLUEBERRY SAUCE

1^1/$_2$ tablespoons arrowroot powder
450g/1lb frozen blueberries, partially thawed
120ml/4fl oz maple syrup
1 teaspoon vanilla extract

> In a small saucepan off the heat, toss the arrowroot with the blueberries until it is mostly dissolved. This takes about 5 minutes; mix occasionally.

> Over medium heat, cook until moisture is released and blueberries are warm. Add the maple syrup and vanilla; heat 5 more minutes, until the sauce thickens a bit.

LEMON CORN WAFFLES WITH BLUEBERRY SAUCE

MAKES 24 REGULAR WAFFLES OR 12–14 BELGIAN WAFFLES

I used to serve these at Sunday brunch at the doghouse, a loft in Brooklyn I once lived in. It was so great to smell these cooking on those freezing cold winter mornings. Yeah, we had no heat, but we compensated with the best vegan waffles you've ever tasted. Serve these with maple syrup and tempeh bacon. This recipe makes a lot of waffles, so feel free to halve it.

275g/10oz plain flour
2¹/2 teaspoons baking powder
¹/2 teaspoon bicarbonate of soda
¹/2 teaspoon salt
2 teaspoons ground cinnamon
1 teaspoon ground ginger
¹/2 teaspoon ground or freshly grated nutmeg
¹/4 teaspoon ground cloves
475ml/16fl oz rice or soy milk
425g/15oz can puréed pumpkin
5 tablespoons oil
65g/2¹/2oz brown sugar
2 teaspoons vanilla extract

> Preheat waffle iron according to the manufacturer's instructions.

> Sift together the flour, baking powder, bicarbonate of soda, salt, and spices. In a separate bowl, vigorously whisk together the soy milk, pumpkin, oil, brown sugar, and vanilla until well emulsified. Pour the wet ingredients into the dry and mix. Prepare the waffles according to the manufacturer's instructions.

MUFFINS AND SCONES

WHENEVER I BAKE MUFFINS I CAN'T HELP BUT SING THE BLACK FLAG SONG "RISE ABOVE." THEN I GET REALLY VEGAN CHEESY AND CHANGE THE LYRICS AROUND: "WE ARE BORN WITH MUFFIN PANS! (RISE ABOVE!) I AM GONNA HAVE MY PAN (RISE ABOVE!)." I CAN'T BELIEVE I JUST TOLD THE WORLD THIS BUT TRY THESE DELICIOUS MUFFINS AND SCONES AND THAT WILL HELP ME SAVE SOME FACE.

MAKES 18 SCONES

This is my basic recipe for scones – they are more like doughy biscuits. I also often make the variations listed below.

350g/12oz plain flour
2 tablespoons baking powder
50g/2oz sugar, plus an extra teaspoon for sprinkling the tops
1/4 teaspoon salt
5 tablespoons vegetable oil
120ml/4floz soy cream (rice or soy milk makes a fine substitution)
175ml/6fl oz rice or soy milk
2 teaspoons cider vinegar

> Preheat oven to 200°C/400°F/gas mark 6. Lightly grease a baking sheet.

> In a large mixing bowl, sift together the flour, baking powder, sugar, and salt. Add the oil, soy cream, rice milk and vinegar. Mix until just combined; the dough should be clumpy and not sticky. Even if there is still a light dusting of flour, that's OK.

> Divide the mixture into 16 equal portions and drop them onto the greased baking sheet and pat the tops just a bit to round them out; sprinkle with a bit of sugar. Bake 12 to 15 minutes, until slightly browned on the bottom and firm on the top.

···❖ **VARIATIONS**

> **Berry Scones:** Fold in 175g/6oz of fresh berries.

> **Chocolate Chip Scones:** Add 1 teaspoon of vanilla extract to the liquid ingredients, add 2 tablespoons of sugar, fold in 150g/5oz chocolate chips.

> **Maple Walnut:** Add 2 teaspoons of maple extract to the liquid ingredients, add 2 tablespoons of sugar, fold in 175g/6oz of walnuts.

MAKES 12 SCONES

I created this recipe specifically for my mom and she was really pleased with how it turned out and so was I. These scones are a little sweeter than normal and they have lots of zesty orange flavour.

120ml/4fl oz soy cream (rice or soy milk make a fine substitution)
175ml/6fl oz rice or soy milk
1 tablespoon cider vinegar
350g/12oz plain flour
65g/2^1/$_2$oz sugar
2 tablespoons baking powder
^{1}/$_4$ teaspoon salt
5 tablespoons vegetable oil
3 tablespoons finely grated orange zest
Orange Glaze (recipe follows)

> Preheat oven to 200°C/400°F/gas mark 6. Lightly grease a baking sheet.

> In a measuring jug combine the soy cream, rice milk, and vinegar.

> In a large mixing bowl, sift together the flour, sugar, baking powder, and salt. Add the rice milk mixture, oil, and orange zest; mix until just combined; the dough should be clumpy and not sticky. Even if there is still a light dusting of flour it's OK.

> Divide the dough in two. Knead one portion a few times, then form into a 15cm/6in disc. Cut the disc into six slices, pizza-style, and place each slice on the prepared baking sheet. Do the same with the remaining dough. Bake for 12 to 15 minutes, until slightly browned on the bottom and firm on top. Transfer to a cooling rack.

> When cool (if they are still only slightly warm that is OK) transfer to parchment paper. Pour about 2 tablespoons Orange Glaze over the scones; let the tops set before eating. If you simply can't wait, prepare to have sticky fingers.

ORANGE GLAZE

115g/4oz icing sugar
2 tablespoons non-hydrogenated margarine, melted
2 tablespoons fresh orange juice
1 teaspoon finely grated orange zest

> Sift the icing sugar into a mixing bowl; add all the other ingredients and mix until smooth.

GLAZED ORANGE SCONES

HAZELNUT SCONES

MAKES 16 SCONES

Ground hazelnuts give these scones a rich texture. A touch of freshly brewed hazelnut coffee elevates them to hazelnut heaven, and the chopped hazelnuts are the icing on the cake (or the hazelnuts on the scone, as the case may be). The scones taste great still warm, topped with margarine and apple butter. I recommend brewing a whole pot of the hazelnut coffee and cooling the rest to have iced hazelnut coffee alongside your scones.

120ml/4fl oz soy cream (use the hazelnut soy cream if you can find it, if not, rice or soy milk makes a fine substitution)
175ml/6fl oz freshly brewed hazelnut coffee
2 teaspoons cider vinegar
1 teaspoon vanilla extract
75g/3oz vegetable shortening
4 tablespoons sugar, plus an extra teaspoon for sprinkling the tops (optional)
225g/8oz plain flour
2 tablespoons baking powder
1/4 teaspoon salt
115g/4oz ground hazelnuts (see Punk Points)
1/2 teaspoon freshly grated nutmeg
50g/2oz toasted and coarsely chopped hazelnuts (see Punk Points)

> Preheat oven to 200°C/400°F/gas mark 6. Lightly grease a baking sheet.

> Measure out the soy cream and coffee and stir in the vinegar and vanilla extract. Set aside.

> In a large bowl, cream together the shortening and sugar.

> In a large mixing bowl, sift together the flour, baking powder, and salt. Add the ground hazelnut and nutmeg. Add the shortening mixture in clumps (use a teaspoon or your fingers) and mix with your fingertips or a pastry knife until the mixture resembles coarse crumbs. Add the coffee mixture and mix with a wooden spoon until just combined; fold in the chopped hazelnuts. The dough should be clumpy and dry; even if there is still a light dusting of flour, that is OK.

> Divide the mixture into 16 equal portions and drop onto the greased baking sheet; sprinkle with a little sugar if you like. Bake 12 to 15 minutes, until slightly browned on the bottom and firm on the top.

> Ground hazelnuts can be bought in supermarkets or you can make your own. To make your own, toast the hazelnuts on a baking sheet at 180°C/350°F/gas mark 4 for about 12 minutes. Wrap the nuts in a kitchen towel for 2 minutes while they are still warm, then rub the nuts together so that any burnt skins come off. (This toasting and peeling method should be used for the toasted, chopped hazelnuts as well.) Transfer the nuts to a strong blender or (better yet) a food processor and pulse into a coarse powder.

LEMON-POPPY SEED MUFFINS

MAKES 1 DOZEN MUFFINS

I made these after asking the visitors on my web site what their favourite muffin was. Turns out it was lemon poppy seed—who knew? I had lots of happy fans after posting this.

200g/7oz plain flour
4 tablespoons sugar
1 tablespoon baking powder
1/4 teaspoon salt
5 tablespoons rapeseed oil
175ml/6fl oz rice or soy milk
175g/6oz soy yogurt, plain or vanilla
    (vanilla will make it only slightly sweeter)
1 teaspoon vanilla extract
2 tablespoons finely grated lemon zest (zest from 2 lemons)
1 tablespoon poppy seeds

> Preheat oven to 200°C/400°F/gas mark 6.

> In a large bowl, sift together the flour, sugar, baking powder, and salt. In a separate bowl, whisk together the oil, rice milk, yogurt, and vanilla. Add the lemon zest to the wet ingredients. Fold the wet ingredients into the dry; halfway through mixing fold in the poppy seeds.

> Spray a twelve-hole muffin tin with nonstick cooking spray. Fill each cup two-thirds full. Bake for 20 to 25 minutes, until a cocktail stick inserted in the centre comes out clean. Serve warm.

···> PUNK POINTS

> To make sure you always have fresh muffins, freeze half a batch. Pour the batter into paper cake cases, then put them in the freezer. Once frozen, store in tightly sealed plastic containers and bake however many you want in a patty tin straight from frozen, adding an extra 8–10 minutes to the cooking time.

MAKES 1 DOZEN MUFFINS

These are my favourite morning muffins. Since I weaned myself off caffeine I need a little kick to wake me up. Actually, I need several really hard kicks and in some cases a bucket of ice water dumped over my head. But what I'm saying is, once I'm awake the little bit of spice to these muffins seals the deal.

75g/3oz raisins
175g/6oz flour
2 teaspoons baking powder
1/2 teaspoon bicarbonate of soda
1/2 teaspoon ground cinnamon
1/4 teaspoon ground or freshly grated nutmeg
4 tablespoons sugar
1/2 teaspoon salt
250ml/8fl oz rice or soy milk
4 tablespoons rapeseed oil
1 teaspoon vanilla extract
4 medium carrots, grated

> Preheat oven to 200°C/400°F/gas mark 6. Spray a twelve-hole muffin tin with nonstick cooking spray or lightly grease with oil.

> Soak the raisins in a bowl of hot water and begin preparing the batter. In a large mixing bowl sift together flour, baking powder, bicarbonate of soda, cinnamon, nutmeg, sugar and salt. Create a well in the centre and add the milk, oil, and vanilla; mix with a wooden spoon until just combined. Fold in the grated carrots. Remove the raisins from the water and fold in.

> Fill the muffin tins three-quarters full. Bake for 18 to 22 minutes, until a cocktail stick or knife inserted in the centre of one comes out clean. Let cool on a cooling rack.

---> PUNK POINTS

Soaking the raisins in hot water gives them new life and makes them plump and juicy. Just boil some water, put the raisins in a bowl, pour the water over them, and let them sit for a good 10 minutes.

 FIZZLE SAYS

While carrots are high in beta-carotene, it is a myth that they actually improve eyesight.

CHERRY-ALMOND MUFFINS

MAKES 1 DOZEN MUFFINS

Cherries are expensive so make sure to pick only the ones that are most perfect and firm. Take your time in the store and go through the whole pile until you come to be known as "Crazy Cherry Girl/Guy" by the shopkeepers.

225g/8oz plain flour
65g/2$^1/_2$oz sugar
2 teaspoons baking powder
$^1/_2$ teaspoon bicarbonate of soda
$^1/_4$ teaspoon salt
5 tablespoons rapeseed oil
175ml/6fl oz rice or soy milk
175g/6oz container soy yogurt, plain or vanilla
   (vanilla will make it only slightly sweeter)
2 teaspoons almond extract
115g/4oz sliced almonds
130g/4$^1/_2$oz fresh cherries, halved and pitted

> Preheat oven to 200°C/400°F/gas mark 6. Lightly grease a twelve-hole muffin tin.

> In a large bowl, sift together flour, sugar, baking powder, bicarbonate of soda, and salt. Create a well in the centre and add the oil, rice milk, yogurt, and almond extract. Mix with a wooden spoon until combined. Fold in half of the almonds and all of the cherries.

> Fill the muffin cups three-quarters full; press the remaining almonds into the tops of the muffins. Bake for 18 to 22 minutes, until a cocktail stick or knife inserted in the centre of one comes out clean.

MAKES 1 DOZEN MUFFINS

These are so tasty and healthy, too.

65g/2$^{1}/_{2}$oz raisins
175g/6oz plain flour
2 teaspoons baking powder
$^{1}/_{2}$ teaspoon bicarbonate of soda
90g/3$^{1}/_{2}$oz sugar
2 teaspoons ground ginger
1 teaspoon ground cinnamon
$^{1}/_{2}$ teaspoon salt
130g/4$^{1}/_{2}$oz bran
300ml/$^{1}/_{2}$ pint rice or soy milk
5 tablespoons rapeseed oil
1 teaspoon vanilla extract
4 tablespoons chopped crystallized ginger

> Preheat oven to 200°C/400°F/gas mark 6. Lightly grease a twelve-hole muffin tin. Soak the raisins in hot water to cover, set aside.

> In a large mixing bowl sift together the flour, baking powder, bicarbonate of soda, sugar, ginger, cinnamon, and salt. Mix in the bran. Create a well in the centre and add the rice milk, oil, and vanilla. Mix with a wooden spoon just until combined. Drain the raisins and fold them in along with the crystallized ginger.

> Fill each muffin cup most of the way full and bake for 20 to 22 minutes, until a cocktail stick or knife inserted in the centre comes out clean.

GINGER-RAISIN BRAN MUFFINS

SUNNY BLUEBERRY-CORN MUFFINS

MAKES 1 DOZEN MUFFINS

These are perfect sweet corn muffins, crispy outside and soft inside. They've got a great crumb, perfect for spreading with a pat of soy margarine. I call them sunny because of the lemon zest.

115g/4oz plain flour
115g/4oz cornmeal
1 tablespoon baking powder
1/2 teaspoon salt
65g/2 1/2 oz sugar
120ml/4fl oz corn or vegetable oil
175ml/6fl oz soy milk
2 tablespoons soy yogurt
1 teaspoon vanilla extract
Finely grated zest of 1 lemon
150g/5oz blueberries

> Preheat oven to 200°C/400°F/gas mark 6. Lightly grease a twelve-hole muffin tin.

> In a large bowl, sift together the flour, cornmeal, baking powder, salt, and sugar. In a separate bowl, whisk together the oil, soy milk, soy yogurt, vanilla, and lemon zest. With a wooden spoon, fold the wet ingredients into the dry. Fold in the blueberries, being careful not to overmix.

> Fill each muffin cup three-quarters full. Bake for 20 to 25 minutes, until a cocktail stick or knife inserted in the centre of one comes out clean. Serve warm.

···❖ PUNK POINTS

> To keep the blueberries from sinking to the bottom of the muffin, toss them around in a bowl of flour to coat. That will give them some "grip" in the batter.

MAKES 1 DOZEN MUFFINS

Here I go and break my own rule and make a muffin that is more like dessert. So sue me. I use powdered instant coffee because I think its coffee flavour remains truer than that of fresh-brewed coffee. If you don't have any instant coffee, just use an extra tablespoon of cocoa powder and have a chocolate-chocolate chip muffin.

175g/6oz plain flour
150g/5oz sugar
25g/1oz cocoa powder
2^1/$_2$ teaspoons baking powder
^{1}/$_2$ teaspoon salt
2 teaspoons instant coffee powder
250ml/8fl oz soy milk
120ml/4fl oz rapeseed oil
3 tablespoons soy yogurt
1 teaspoon vanilla extract
65g/2^1/$_2$oz chocolate chips

> Preheat oven to 190°C/375°F/gas mark 5. Lightly grease a twelve-hole muffin tin.

> In a large bowl, sift together flour, sugar, cocoa powder, baking powder, and salt. Mix in the instant coffee powder.

> In a separate bowl, whisk together the soy milk, oil, yogurt, and vanilla.

> Pour the wet ingredients into the dry and mix until the dry ingredients are moistened. Fold in the chocolate chips. Fill the muffin cups three-quarters full. Bake 18 to 20 minutes, or until a cocktail stick or knife inserted into the centre of one comes out clean.

MOCHA CHIP MUFFINS

THE BEST PUMPKIN MUFFINS

MAKES 1 DOZEN MUFFINS

Everyone loves these muffins. (You think I throw around phrases like "The Best" for nothing?) I created them when I was baking for a café and they sold like nobody's business. They truly are perfect in every way.

200g/7oz plain flour
250g/9oz sugar
1 tablespoon baking powder
1/4 teaspoon salt
1 teaspoon ground cinnamon
1/2 teaspoon ground or freshly grated nutmeg
1/2 teaspoon ground ginger
1/4 teaspoon ground allspice
1/8 teaspoon ground cloves
250ml/8fl oz puréed pumpkin
   (fresh or from a can)
120ml/4fl oz soy milk
120ml/4fl oz vegetable oil
2 tablespoons molasses

> Preheat oven to 200°C/400°F/gas mark 6. Lightly grease a twelve-hole muffin tin.

> Sift together flour, sugar, baking powder, salt, and spices. In a separate bowl, whisk together pumpkin, soy milk, oil, and molasses. Pour the wet ingredients into the dry and mix.

> Fill the muffin cups two-thirds full. Bake for 18 to 20 minutes, until a cocktail stick or knife inserted in the centre comes out clean.

···❖ VARIATION

Fold in 115g/4oz chopped fresh cranberries or chopped walnuts, or a mixture of the two.

MAKES 1 DOZEN MUFFINS

The grated and chopped apples create an apple pie filling in the centre of the muffin. It's a nice surprise to an already sweet and spicy treat.

For muffins:
175g/6oz flour
75g/3oz sugar
1 teaspoon baking powder
1 teaspoon bicarbonate of soda
1 teaspoon ground cinnamon
1/2 teaspoon ground allspice
1/8 teaspoon ground cloves
1/4 teaspoon salt
175ml/6fl oz cider
5 tablespoons rapeseed oil
1 teaspoon vanilla extract
115g/4oz grated apple
50g/2oz chopped apple (5mm/1/4in pieces)

For topping:
4 tablespoons plain flour
4 tablespoons brown sugar
1/2 teaspoon ground cinnamon
1/4 teaspoon ground allspice
Pinch of salt
3 tablespoons rapeseed oil

> Prepare the topping by mixing all the dry topping ingredients together in a small bowl. Drizzle the oil in while mixing with your fingertips until crumbs form. Set aside.

> Preheat oven to 190°C/375°F/gas mark 5, lightly grease a twelve-hole muffin tin.

> In a large mixing bowl, sift together the flour, sugar, baking powder, bicarbonate of soda, spices, and salt. Create a well in the centre and add the cider, oil, and vanilla. Mix, then fold in the grated and chopped apple.

> Fill each muffin cup two-thirds full. Sprinkle the crumb topping over each muffin. Bake for 22 minutes.

APPLE PIE-CRUMB CAKE MUFFINS

SOUPS

SOMETIMES I DOUBLE THESE RECIPES
AND MAKE A BIG BATCH TO EITHER FREEZE
OR EAT THROUGHOUT THE WEEK. I LOVE
MAKING SOUP FOR SEVERAL REASONS,
LIKE IT'S DELICIOUS AND FAST, BUT THE
BIGGEST IMPETUS IS THAT EVERYTHING
GOES IN ONE POT AND THERE AREN'T A
LOAD OF DISHES TO CLEAN UP (OR LET SIT
IN THE SINK FOR A WEEK) AFTERWARDS.
ALL OF THESE SOUP RECIPES ARE HEARTY
ENOUGH TO BE MEALS, WITH SOME RICE
OR GOOD CRUSTY BREAD.

CARROT BISQUE

I've never been crazy about carrot soups, they always seemed a little too skimpy and health-foody for me. But this slightly sweet, incredibly creamy and hearty carrot soup changed all that. It's easy to make, to boot.

1.3kg/3lb carrots, peeled and diced into a little smaller
    than 1cm/^{1}/$_2$in pieces
1 large onion, chopped
2 tablespoons groundnut oil (vegetable oil will do)
2 cloves garlic, finely chopped
1 tablespoon curry powder
^{1}/$_2$ teaspoon salt
A few dashes fresh black pepper
750ml/1^1/$_4$ pints vegetable stock,
    or 1 bouillon cube dissolved in 750ml/1^1/$_4$ pints water
375g/13oz can coconut milk
1 tablespoon maple syrup

> In a stockpot over low-medium heat, cook the carrots and onions in the groundnut oil for 7 to 10 minutes; cover and stir occasionally. You want the onions to brown but not to burn, although if they burn a little bit it's not the end of the world. Add the garlic, curry, salt, and pepper; sauté for 1 more minute. Add the 750ml/1^1/$_4$ pints of stock, cover, and bring to a boil. Lower the heat and simmer for 10 to 12 minutes, or until the carrots are tender.

> Add the coconut milk and bring to a low boil. Turn the heat off. Use a handheld blender to purée half of the soup; if you don't have one, then purée half the soup in a blender and add it back to the soup pot (see Punk Point). Add the maple syrup and stir. Serve hot.

---⁞ PUNK POINT

> If you are using a blender to purée the soup, let the soup cool a bit so that the steam doesn't cause the blender lid to pop off and hot soup to splatter everywhere. Once the soup has cooled, give it a few pulses in the blender, lift the lid to let steam escape, and repeat.

Fresh sweetcorn, especially in the summer when it's in season, has such a pure taste I sometimes just like to eat it raw. Potatoes give this soup a creamy, hearty body and the jalapeños give it just a little kick.

1 tablespoon olive oil
1 medium-size onion, cut into 5mm/1/4in dice
1 large red pepper, finely chopped
2 carrots, peeled and cut into 1cm/1/2in dice
2 jalapeño chillies, seeded and thinly sliced
   (use just one if you like less heat)
1 teaspoon dried rosemary
1 teaspoon dried thyme
A few dashes fresh black pepper
1 teaspoon salt
750ml/1 1/2 pints vegetable stock or water
475g/1lb 2oz fresh sweetcorn kernels (from about 5 cobs of sweetcorn)
2 medium-size potatoes, peeled and sliced into 1cm/1/2in chunks
1 bay leaf
Pinch cayenne
Juice of 1 lime
4 tablespoons plain soy milk
1 tablespoon maple syrup

> In a stockpot sauté the onions, peppers, carrots, and jalapeños in the olive oil over medium heat until the onions are translucent, about 7 minutes. Add rosemary, thyme, black pepper, and salt; sauté 1 minute more. Add the stock, sweetcorn, potatoes, bay leaf, and cayenne. Cover and bring to a boil, then lower the heat and simmer for 20 minutes, or until the potatoes are tender. Uncover and simmer 10 minutes more to let the liquid reduce a bit.

> Remove the bay leaf and purée half the chowder either using a handheld blender or by transferring half the chowder to a blender, puréeing till smooth (see Punk Point), and adding back to soup. Add the lime juice to taste, and the soy milk and maple syrup, and simmer 5 more minutes. Let sit for at least 10 minutes and serve. Tastes even better the next day.

⋯⟩ PUNK POINT

> If you are using a blender to purée the soup, let the soup cool a bit so that the steam doesn't cause the blender lid to pop off and hot soup to splatter everywhere. Once the soup has cooled, give it a few pulses in the blender, lift the lid to let steam escape, and repeat.

SERVES 6-8

Eating this soup makes me think I am in Mother Russia in the late nineteenth century; I've come home after strolling the promenade in Saint Petersburg and I'm getting ready to complete the next chapter of my tragic novel, but first—soup.

2 tablespoons olive oil
1 large onion, finely chopped
3 cloves garlic
2 teaspoons dried tarragon
A few dashes fresh black pepper
1.75 litres/3 pints water
4 medium-size beetroot, peeled, cut in half, sliced 5mm/1/4in thick
165g/6oz pearl barley
3 tablespoons tamari
425g/15oz can black soybeans, rinsed and drained
2 tablespoons balsamic vinegar
25g/1oz chopped fresh dill
Pumpernickel Croûtons (recipe follows)

> In a stockpot over medium heat, sauté the onion in the olive oil for 5 minutes. Add the garlic, tarragon, and pepper; sauté until fragrant (about a minute). Add 1.75 litres/3 pints water, the beetroot, barley, and tamari, cover, and bring to a boil. Lower the heat and simmer for 30 minutes. Add the beans and simmer for another 10 to 15 minutes, stirring frequently to prevent the barley from sticking together, or until the barley is tender. Add the balsamic vinegar and fresh dill. Serve with Pumpernickel Croûtons, and garnish with more fresh dill.

PUMPERNICKEL CROÛTONS

2 tablespoons extra-virgin olive oil
1/2 teaspoon dried tarragon
1/4 teaspoon salt
4 slices firm pumpernickel bread, cut into 5mm/1/4in dice

> Preheat oven to 200°C/400°F/gas mark 6.

> In a wide, shallow bowl, stir together the olive oil, tarragon, and salt. Add the diced bread and toss gently to coat. Spread the bread in a single layer on a baking sheet, toast for 8 to 10 minutes, stirring once. Remove from oven and let cool.

SERVES 6

This is one of the recipes that you can really mess around with; add courgette or cauliflower or other vegetables and try different beans; I also like to add tempeh or frozen and thawed tofu sometimes, as you add the potatoes. Let the soup sit for at least 10 minutes before serving—the longer, the better. If you want to make the soup less spicy, remove the seeds from the chipotles before using.

2 tablespoons olive oil
1 large onion, quartered and thinly sliced
3 cloves garlic
2 teaspoons ground cumin
$1/2$ teaspoon salt
A few dashes fresh black pepper
2 canned chipotle chillies, drained and chopped
2 x 400g cans crushed tomatoes
750ml/$11/4$ pints water
4 potatoes, cut into 2cm/$3/4$in dice
2 carrots, peeled, cut into 2cm/$3/4$in dice
175g/6oz sweetcorn (if using fresh, it's 2 cobs)
450g/1lb can black beans, drained and rinsed
40g/$11/2$oz fresh coriander, lightly packed, torn into pieces (stems and all)
Finely grated zest of 1 lime
Juice of 1 lime

> In a stockpot, sauté the onions in the oil over moderate heat for 5 minutes. Add the garlic, cumin, salt, and black pepper. Sauté 1 minute more. Add the chipotles, tomatoes and water, stir. Add the potatoes and carrots, cover, bring to a low boil, and simmer for 20 minutes.

> Uncover, add the sweetcorn and beans. Thin with more water if needed. Cook uncovered for 5 more minutes. Add the coriander, lime zest, and lime juice. Let sit for at least 10 minutes. Serve. (If you can wait an hour to eat it, it tastes so good when it's had a chance to sit around and is gently reheated.)

···> **PUNK POINTS**

> Be very careful when working with hot chillies, the white lining in the chilli contains a chemical called capsaicin, which gives it its heat. Don't ever touch the inside of the chilli with your bare hands and then your eyes or they will burn for hours and sometimes even the next day. Either work very carefully with a small paring knife or wear a pair of disposable gloves while cutting and chopping.

CHIPOTLE, SWEETCORN, AND BLACK BEAN STEW

ROASTED BUTTERNUT SQUASH SOUP

SERVES 6

Roasting the squash intensifies its sweetness but be careful not to eat it all before you have a chance to make the soup. The ingredients here are simple yet the results are scrumptious.

2.25kg/5lb butternut squash, peeled, bulbous part cut from the stem part, then each part sliced in half, seeds removed
4 tablespoons olive oil
1 medium-size yellow onion, diced
1 serrano chilli, chopped
(any chilli will do, or you can omit if you don't want it spicy at all)
1 tablespoon grated fresh ginger
3 cloves garlic, finely chopped
1 teaspoon salt (or more to taste)
1 litre/1¾ pints vegetable stock, or 2 cubes vegetable bouillon dissolved in 1 litre/1¾ pints water
1 tablespoon maple syrup
Juice of 1 or 2 limes, to taste

> Preheat oven to 220°C/425°F/gas mark 7.

> Lightly coat the squash halves with 2 tablespoons of the olive oil and place cut side down on a nonstick or parchment-lined baking tin. Bake for 40 to 45 minutes, or until the squash is tender and easily pierced with a fork.

> When the squash is about 15 minutes from being done, in a stockpot over medium heat sauté the onions in the remaining 2 tablespoons of olive oil for 5 minutes. Add the chillies; sauté 5 minutes more. Lastly, add the ginger, garlic, and salt; sauté 2 minutes more.

> When the squash is ready, purée in a blender or food processor along with the vegetable stock and sautéed onion, until smooth. Return the mixture to the pot and heat through, add the maple syrup and lime juice, and serve.

⇢ PUNK POINTS

> My top-secret technique for preparing a butternut squash: First, peel the whole thing with a serrated peeler, if you have one -it does a good job of slicing off the hard skin. Cut the squash in half widthwise, separating the bulbous part from the long part. Place the bulbous part cut-side down and slice it in half, then use a tablespoon to remove the seeds and the stringy bits. You should then be able to cut the squash into smaller pieces. Next, slice the long part of the squash in half and then cut into whatever size pieces you need.
All too often I watch people struggle with this gourd, trying to cut it in half in one fell swoop and then peel it. I hope this has cleared things up for those of you who don't like cooking butternut squash because it's too difficult.

FOOD NOT BOMBS

Food Not Bombs is a loosely knit network of activists that get together on a regular basis to cook food and feed people. Groups exist all across the world. Much more than Meals on Wheels, it's a social movement that has been growing since 1980.

In the late '80s and early '90s, a group of us would get together on Sundays and go from store to store gathering food donations. In many cases, it was food that would otherwise have been discarded—blemished vegetables from the greengrocers or day-old bagels from the bagel shops. We'd haul everything over to Lucky 13— a squat on 13th Street that had been around forever and was cool enough to host punk shows and let strangers use their kitchen—in a shopping trolley "donated" by the local Key Food. There we would concoct hearty vats of vegetarian soup over a few hot plates, using water we tapped from the fire hydrant down the block (I'm not kidding).

When the soups were done, everything would be piled back into the shopping trolley and rolled a few blocks to Tompkins Square Park. The crowd we fed was diverse: yippies, homeless, junkies, psychopaths, artists, squatters, punks, and some combinations of the above. This was during the time of the Tompkins Square Park riots; activists were fighting to keep a curfew off the park and a shantytown called Tent City was set up on the lawn as a home for dozens of people. It was a rather dystopian scene. Cops milled about, and it was anyone's guess as to whether they would decide to arrest us on a given evening. Despite these drawbacks, conversation was always lively and the food was always appreciated.

One of the greatest things about Food Not Bombs was that you could go to virtually any city and get involved. The experience was always different from place to place. In San Francisco I was shocked to see how organized they were. They had a van! They had folding tables and a banner! In Berkeley they cooked in a college dorm and served scones that were donated by a bakery. In Minneapolis they seemed to serve exclusively punks. In Baltimore they served in the inner cities and I bore witness to the sort of urban decay usually saved for post-apocalyptic movies.

If I had to name a time and place, I would say that cooking for FNB was where I gained my knife skills as I chopped scores and scores of vegetables. It also influenced my cooking for years to come. For a long time it was nearly impossible for me to cook normal portions of food.

It is easy to start your own Food Not Bombs, or join an existing one, and feed people in your community. Check their web site for more information: **www.foodnotbombs.com**.

If distributed equally, the world produces enough food to feed everyone. There is an abundance of food. In fact, in the US, every day, in every city, far more edible food is discarded than is needed to feed those who do not have enough to eat.

Consider this. Before food reaches your table, it is produced and handled by farmers, coops, manufacturers, distributors, wholesalers, and retailers. At every step, some perfectly edible food is discarded for a variety of business reasons. In the average city, approximately 10% of all solid waste is food. Nationally, this is an incredible total of 46 billion pounds per year, just under 200 pounds per person per year . . .

From the Food Not Bombs web site

POTATO-ASPARAGUS SOUP

SERVES 6

I didn't spice this up too much because asparagus is my favourite vegetable and I like its flavour to shine through. I like to add some fresh dill to each serving but it's completely optional. If you like a chunkier soup, then just purée half of the soup, or use a handheld blender and purée to your liking.

1.3kg/3lb potatoes, peeled, cut into 2.5cm/1in chunks
450g/1lb asparagus, rough ends discarded,
    tips cut into 5cm/2in pieces, lower part cut into 1cm/1/2in pieces
2 tablespoons olive oil
1 large onion, cut into 1cm/1/2in dice
3 cloves garlic, finely chopped
1 teaspoon salt
A few dashes fresh black pepper
1 litre/1 3/4 pints vegetable stock,
    or 2 bouillon cubes dissolved in 1 litre/1 3/4 pints water
2 bay leaves
Juice of 1 lemon
15g/1/2oz chopped fresh dill

> Place potatoes in a stockpot and cover with cold water. Cover the pot and bring to a boil, then lower the heat and simmer for 20 minutes or until tender. Add the asparagus, boil for 3 minutes, drain, and set aside.

> Rinse out the pot, then in the same pot sauté the onion in the olive oil for 5 to 7 minutes; add the garlic, salt and black pepper, and sauté 2 more minutes. Add the stock and bay leaves, boil for 10 minutes, discard the bay leaves. Add the potatoes and asparagus, heat through, then purée three-quarters of the soup in a blender or food processor (see Punk Point). Reheat if necessary. Add a squeeze of lemon and serve garnished with fresh dill.

⋯⊹ **PUNK POINT**

> If you are using a blender to purée the soup, let the soup cool a bit so that the steam doesn't cause the blender lid to pop off and hot soup to splatter everywhere. Once the soup has cooled, give it a few pulses in the blender, lift the lid to let steam escape, and repeat.

SERVES 6

Serve this with garlic croûtons or a nice peasant bread. When you eat this soup you will be transported to a rustic villa in Italy where the air is clean and fresh, the locals are provincial but friendly, and you have the solitude you need to finish your sonnets. If you have never roasted garlic before, you don't know what you are missing; it adds a great depth of flavour. I like to think of it as a "restaurant taste" for lack of a better phrase.

2 tablespoons olive oil
1 medium-size onion, chopped
1 teaspoon salt
A few dashes fresh black pepper
1/2 teaspoon fennel seeds, crushed
1 litre/1 3/4 pints vegetable stock, or 2 bouillon cubes dissolved
    in 1 litre/1 3/4 pints water
450g/1lb cooked cannellini beans, drained or canned beans,
    drained and rinsed
3 fresh sage leaves, chopped
1 bay leaf
Juice of 1/2 lemon, or to taste
2 heads garlic, roasted (see Punk Points)

> In a stockpot over medium-high heat sauté the onions in the olive oil for 5 to 7 minutes.

> Add the salt, black pepper, and fennel seeds; sauté for 1 minute. Add the stock, beans, sage, and bay leaf, bring to a boil, then lower the heat and simmer uncovered for 5 minutes. Remove the bay leaf. Add the roasted garlic and purée in batches in a blender or preferably a food processor (see Punk Point). Return to the pot and add lemon juice. Serve garnished with fresh fennel leaves if you have some, and/or some peeled carrot and/or parsley.

⋯⁘ **PUNK POINT**

> **To roast garlic:** Preheat oven to 180°C/350°F/gas mark 4. Peel off as much of the papery skin as you can and put the garlic in the oven for about 30 minutes. Remove from oven and, when cool, squeeze the garlic out or peel the skin away from each clove.

WHITE BEAN AND ROASTED GARLIC SOUP

CHILLI SIN CARNE AL MOLE

SERVES 6–8

This is Terry Hope Romero's recipe and I am a better woman for having tried it. The chocolate gives the chilli a traditional mole flavour that is otherworldly. Terry tells us, "I like thick, chunky bean and vegetable-filled vegetarian chilli as much as the next guy, but I've always had a longing for a meatless version of the more traditional Mexican-style chilli con carne—a dark red stock, large chunks of meat, accompanied only by a few bits of onions, chillies, and spices. Seitan is ideal for this recipe, but being a meatless version it would seem rather stark without the addition of good old pinto beans. The consistency is more like a very chunky, thick soup than your usual stew-like chilli. Like most soups and stews, this chilli tastes even better reheated the next day."

5 tablespoons olive oil
1 large onion, chopped
1 small jalapeño chilli, finely chopped
1 small red pepper, chopped
3 cloves garlic, smashed
450g/1lb seitan, coarsley chopped into 5mm/1/4in cubes
2 tablespoons chilli powder
1 teaspoon ground cinnamon
1/2 teaspoon ground cumin
2 x 400g/14oz cans whole, peeled tomatoes in sauce
3 tablespoons cocoa powder
3 tablespoons molasses
2 x 400g cans pinto beans, drained and well rinsed
600ml/1 pint vegetable stock

> Preheat a large pot (at least 7 litres/12 pints) over medium-high heat; pour in and heat the olive oil. Add the onions and peppers and sauté for 2 minutes; then add the garlic and seitan. Cook for 8 minutes, until onions are soft. Add the chilli powder, cinnamon, and cumin, stirring constantly for another minute. Add the tomatoes, cocoa powder, and molasses. Stir and break up the tomatoes with back of a spoon, then add the beans and vegetable stock. Cover and bring to a gentle boil, then lower the heat and simmer for about 30 minutes. Allow to sit at least 20 minutes before serving.

SERVES 6–8

This is a nice and simple yet flavourful soup. Serve it as a main course with some jasmine rice or as the perfect starter to an Indian meal. You will be surprised and relieved at how easy it is to prepare.

1 tablespoon olive oil
1 medium-size white onion, cut into 5mm/¼in dice
3 cloves garlic, finely chopped
2 tablespoons fresh ginger, finely chopped
2 teaspoons curry powder
1 teaspoon ground cumin
¼ teaspoon ground coriander
¼ teaspoon ground cardamom
A generous pinch cinnamon
2 teaspoons salt
1.75 litres/3 pints water
450g/1lb dried split peas
1 carrot
Fresh coriander for garnish (optional)

> In a stockpot, sauté the onions in the olive oil over medium heat for about 5 minutes. Add the garlic, ginger, spices, and salt. Sauté for 2 more minutes.

> Add the water and stir well. Add the split peas. Cover and bring to a boil.

> Bring heat back down to medium; simmer for about an hour, until the peas are tender. Grate in the carrot and serve. You can garnish with fresh coriander if you have it on hand.

CURRIED SPLIT PEA SOUP

MATZOH BALL SOUP

SERVES 8

I could write a novel on everything it took for me to perfect this recipe, but instead I will just give you the beautiful results. These are perfect, light, fluffy, and flavourful matzoh dumplings. Use homemade vegetable stock to add tons of love and flavour. I suggest making the Vegetable Stock (page 76) the night before. You can even make the matzoh mixture the night before, and the big day will be a breeze.

You can halve the recipe or even third it if you like. If you don't have a huge stockpot (I use a 11 litre/19 pint) then halve the recipe or boil the matzoh balls in two sessions. I make my own matzoh meal by grinding the matzoh in a food processor (it takes about six sheets to get the 175g/6oz called for in this recipe) but shop-bought will work just as well.

175g/6oz matzoh meal
3/4 teaspoon salt, plus extra for the boiling water
3/4 teaspoon ground black pepper
350g/12oz firm silken tofu
2 litres/3.5 pints or so Rich Vegetable Stock (recipe follows)
5 tablespoons extra-virgin olive oil
1 carrot, peeled
A handful fresh dill, coarsely chopped
Fresh parsley for garnish

> In a mixing bowl, combine the matzoh meal with the salt and pepper; set aside.

> Crumble the tofu into a blender or food processor, add 120ml/4fl oz of the vegetable stock, and purée until smooth. Add the oil and blend again.

> Mix the tofu mixture with the matzoh meal, making sure that everything is moist. Grate half the carrot into the mixture and mix until it's well distributed. Cover the bowl with clingfilm and refrigerate for at least an hour and up to overnight. You can't skip this step; it's important in making sure that the matzoh balls will not fall apart when boiled.

> When you are ready to form the balls, fill a large stockpot with enough water to fit all the matzoh balls with minimal touching. Salt the water generously, cover, and bring to a boil.

> Set out a chopping board upon which to line up the formed matzoh balls, and cover it with parchment paper if you have any, to prevent sticking. Also have handy a wet cloth to wipe your hands on between forming each matzoh ball.

> Remove the matzoh mixture from the fridge. Form into tightly packed, walnut-size balls and place on the prepared chopping board. When all the balls are prepared, drop carefully into the boiling water, one or two at a time, with a spatula or slotted spoon. Take your time and be careful not to plop one on top of another; they need to remain separate. When all the balls are in the water, cover the pot and DO NOT LIFT LID FOR FORTY MINUTES! Sorry for the caps, just had to stress it. When the 40 minutes are up, you can remove the lid. The matzoh balls will have floated to the top and will drop back down when the lid is lifted. This is fun to watch.

> Now they are ready to serve; however, to make them even lighter, you can turn off the heat, cover the pot again, and let them sit in the water for another hour or so. This way they absorb more water and expand a bit more.

> Prepare the remaining stock by placing it in a separate pot. Grate the other half of the carrot into the stock, along with a healthy handful of fresh dill. Bring to a low boil, and when it's just heated you're ready to prepare the bowls.

> With a slotted spoon, carefully remove the matzoh balls from their pot and place two or three in each bowl. Ladle the stock over the matzoh balls, so that they're covered only about halfway. You can garnish with some more fresh dill, or parsley. Serve to whomever you love.

> If you are not serving the soup right away, you can refrigerate the matzoh balls overnight, and boil them when ready to prepare the soup. Some people even freeze leftovers, but I never have as there've never been leftovers.

RICH VEGETABLE STOCK

MAKES ABOUT 2 LITRES/3.5 PINTS

I make this stock to use with my matzoh ball soup. You can use other veggies, such as celery, squash, potatoes, or mushrooms; just make sure there is enough water to cover everything. Keep the skins on the onions for added colour and flavour. You can also try other herbs, like thyme, rosemary, bay leaves, and peppercorns, for a stronger stock.

1 tablespoon olive oil
1 large onion, skin included, coarsely chopped
2 large carrots, peeled and coarsely chopped
2 parsnips, peeled and coarsely chopped
3 cloves garlic, smashed
2 leeks, well rinsed and coarsely chopped
40g/1^{1}/$_{2}$oz fresh parsley
40g/1^{1}/$_{2}$oz fresh dill
2.3 litres/4 pints water
1 teaspoon salt

> In a large stockpot, heat the oil. Sauté the onions for about 5 minutes on medium heat. Add all other ingredients and bring to a boil. Reduce the heat and let simmer for 1^{1}/$_{2}$ hours, uncovered.

> Let the stock cool till it's an OK temperature to handle. Strain into a large bowl through muslin or a very fine-mesh sieve. Press the vegetables with a gentle but firm pressure to get all the moisture out.

> This will keep in the fridge in a tightly sealed container for up to 3 days, or freeze for up to 3 months.

LITTLE MEALS, SANDWICHES, AND FINGER FOOD

THESE CAN BE CONSIDERED APPETIZERS, SNACKS, OR IN SOME CASES HORS D'OEUVRES. THEY ARE ALL GREAT THINGS TO BRING TO A FRIENDS OR TO COOK WHEN YOU HAVE PEOPLE OVER FOR BOARD GAME NIGHT (EVERYONE HAS A BOARD GAME NIGHT, RIGHT? OR AM I JUST GETTING OLD?).

FRESH SWEETCORN FRITTERS

MAKES 15 FRITTERS

These are really fast and yummy. The jalapeño and red pepper make the pancakes colourful and add just a little spice. If you don't have a red pepper laying around, just leave it out. Serve with salsa or as a breakfast side dish in place of potatoes. A cast iron frying pan works best for even frying.

175g/6oz extra-firm silken tofu
1 tablespoon pure maple syrup
2 tablespoons soy milk
4 tablespoons plain flour
3 cobs sweetcorn, kernels cut from the cob (see Punk Points)
  (about 250g/9oz)
1/4 teaspoon salt
Several dashes fresh black pepper
1 jalapeño, very finely chopped
1/4 red pepper, very finely chopped
Corn oil for frying (rapeseed or any light vegetable oil will do)

> In a blender or food processor whiz the tofu, maple syrup, and soy milk, scraping down the sides with a rubber spatula often, until everything is smooth. Add half the sweetcorn and pulse about 20 times (scraping down the sides after 10 times), so that the mixture is chunky. Transfer to a bowl, add the rest of the ingredients (except for the oil), and combine well.

> Heat a thin layer of oil in a heavy frying pan over medium-high. Drop the batter by tablespoonfuls into the frying pan. Flatten a little with the back of the spoon (wet the spoon first to avoid sticking). Cook 2 1/2 to 3 minutes on each side, until lightly browned. I do this in two batches. When done, rest them on kitchen paper to drain the oil.

···❖ PUNK POINTS

> To cut the sweetcorn from the cob, place the sweetcorn pointy side up on a kitchen towel or kitchen paper. Take a chef's knife and cut downward, as close as you can to the cob. The towel will keep the sweetcorn kernels from bouncing everywhere and also makes a handy vehicle for transporting them to the mixing bowl.

MY CHILDHOOD IN YELLOW CABS AND KNISHES

When I was a child, my father was a NYC cabbie. Like so many children of divorced parents I only saw him on the weekends but the thing was he worked on the weekends, so I got to drive around in the taxi with him. He would stack two phone books on the front seat for me to sit on, so that I could look out the window. This was the NYC I loved as a child: bright, dangerous, and loud. Looking out the window was like watching a movie, so many different kinds of people. My dad cursed at most of the passengers when they'd give a lousy tip, which made the rides even more colourful for me. At the time the Lower East Side was still teeming with Jewish culture and my dad knew all the best places for a quick nosh. Among them was Yonah Shimmel knishes on Houston Street.

Today the neighbourhood is pretty much a hipster shopping mall but miraculously Yonah Shimmel is still there, and its delicious knishes still line the window. I think of my dad whenever I pass and I long for that NYC I knew as a child. I can only imagine the NYC my parents remember. I like to stop in once in a while and get nostalgic for a time that I knew and those old days that I didn't know.

MAKES 15 GOOD-SIZE KNISHES

I brought these to dinner at my aunt's one year and everyone loved them until she started telling people that they were vegan, then all of a sudden no one would touch them. Actually, most knish recipes are vegan. I like to make all three fillings because it's easy to do and the colours look really cool together. The real work here is the dough, which you have to knead for a long time to get it smooth and stretchy enough; after that you are halfway to knish madness. There are a lot of steps but actually not so much active preparation or cooking time, so don't be intimidated.

For the dough:
1 medium-size potato
2 tablespoons olive oil, plus extra for brushing
175ml/6fl oz cold water
1 teaspoon salt
1 teaspoon baking powder
350g/12oz plain flour

For the fillings:
1 large yellow onion, finely chopped
4 tablespoons olive oil
6 medium-size potatoes
1 teaspoon salt
1/4 teaspoon ground black pepper
275g/10oz frozen spinach, thawed and drained
    (drain while potatoes bake)
4 medium-size sweet potatoes (about 900g/2lb)
1/4 teaspoon ground or freshly grated nutmeg
1/4 teaspoon ground cinnamon
1/4 teaspoon ground allspice

> Preheat oven to 180°C/350°F/gas mark 4. Prick the seven regular potatoes with a fork and wrap in foil and place in the oven. The four sweet potatoes can just go in as is. Take out the sweet potatoes after 40 minutes; the regular potatoes will need to bake another 30 minutes, so they will take about 70 minutes total, depending on their size. Remove from the oven and let cool.

To make the dough:

> In a large bowl, place one peeled baked potato for the dough, let the others continue to cool. Add the oil and water to the potato and mash until well combined. Add the salt and baking powder, and then add

the flour in batches, kneading with each addition. Knead until you have a smooth dough. This can take up to 15 minutes, so have someone nearby to help knead in case your little hands get tired. Let the dough rest while you prepare the fillings.

For potato knishes:

> Sauté the onions in 2 tablespoons of the olive oil over medium heat for 15 minutes, until browned and slightly caramelized.

> Mash the six peeled, baked potatoes in a large bowl. Add the cooked onions, the remaining 2 tablespoons of olive oil, and salt and pepper to taste. Mash together well.

For spinach knishes:

> Add the thawed, drained spinach to half of the potato mixture and mix until well combined.

For sweet potato knishes:

> Mash the baked sweet potatoes. Add 1/4 teaspoon each ginger, nutmeg, cinnamon and salt, and mix well.

To assemble and bake the knishes:

> Cut the dough into three equal portions. Roll one portion out as thinly as possible, into a 35 x 15cm/14 x 6in rectangle. It won't be a perfect rectangle, more of an oval, and that is fine. Sprinkle with flour as you roll to keep the dough unsticky.

> Place 200g/7oz of a single filling down the centre of the rolled-out portion of dough. Spread out so that the filling is roughly 30 x 5cm/12 x 2 in. Fold the dough over the filling the long way to create a roll. Trim the ends of the roll up to where the filling begins. Place folded side down on lightly greased baking sheet.

> Repeat with the other two portions of dough and the other two fillings. (You may have extra filling, depending on how big your potatoes were. Don't overstuff the knishes, just bite the bullet and eat the filling on its own.)

> With a knife, score each roll into fifths. That will give them a nice shape and make them easier to cut when they are done. Brush each lightly with olive oil. Bake at 180°C/350°F/gas mark 4 for 40 minutes.

> Remove from oven; let cool just enough so that you can slice them. Serve warm, with plenty of mustard for the potato and spinach ones.

OLIVE, TOMATO, AND MILLET STUFFED COURGETTES

SERVES 8

Courgette boats are perfect vehicles for transporting the tangy olive-tomato-millet combination into your mouth.

1 medium-size onion, finely chopped
1 tablespoon olive oil
2 cloves garlic, finely chopped
75g/3oz millet, rinsed
A few dashes fresh black pepper
1/2 teaspoon dried rosemary
1/2 teaspoon dried thyme
1/2 teaspoon dried marjoram
1/2 teaspoon dried basil
1 teaspoon paprika
1/2 teaspoon salt
600g/1lb 6oz can whole tomatoes
475ml/6fl oz vegetable stock or water
4 medium-size courgettes, ends trimmed
50g/2oz chopped, pitted kalamata olives
4 tablespoons capers
Chopped fresh parsley for garnish

> Sauté the onions in the olive oil over moderate heat for 5 to 7 minutes, until the onions are translucent. Add the garlic and sauté until fragrant, about a minute.

> Add the millet, herbs, spices, and salt; sauté for about 3 minutes. Add the tomatoes, crushing with your hands as you add them. Add the remaining tomato juice and vegetable stock. Cover the pot and bring to a boil, then lower the heat and simmer for 20 minutes.

> Meanwhile, prepare the courgettes: Slice in half lengthwise. Place in a large saucepan cut side down, fill the pan with enough water to cover the courgettes halfway. Cover the pan, bring to a boil, then cook for 5 minutes. Remove the courgettes from the water and place on a plate to cool. Once cool enough to handle, use a tablespoon to remove their pulp, leaving only about 5mm/1/4in of pulp in the courgette. Chop the removed pulp and reserve.

> Preheat oven to 180°C/350°F/gas mark 4.

> Add the courgette pulp, olives, and capers to the millet mixture. Simmer for about 5 more minutes, until the millet is tender.

> Stuff each courgette half with some mixture. Place in a baking dish and bake for about 20 minutes. Let cool about 5 minutes before serving.

MAKES 36 SMALL SAMOSAS OR 18 LARGE ONES

Samosas are crispy pockets of dough, stuffed with a rich and flavourful filling. I can't imagine starting any Indian meal without them. The samosas I make are baked not fried, and I opt to use soy beans instead of peas for a more toothsome bite, although you can stick with green peas if you're all about tradition. Serve with Coconut-Mint Chutney (recipe follows).

For the dough:

175ml/6fl oz rice or soy milk
4 tablespoons vegetable oil
1 tablespoon cider vinegar (any mild vinegar will do)
About 350g/12oz plain flour
1/4 teaspoon ground turmeric
1/4 teaspoon baking powder
1 teaspoon salt

For the filling:

3 medium-size potatoes, peeled and cut into 2.5cm/1in chunks
2 tablespoons vegetable oil plus extra for brushing
1 teaspoon cumin seeds
2 teaspoons mustard seeds
1 medium-size yellow onion, very finely chopped
2 carrots, finely diced
2 cloves garlic, finely chopped
1 tablespoon fresh ginger, finely chopped
1 teaspoon ground coriander
1/2 teaspoon ground turmeric
Pinch of cayenne pepper
1 teaspoon salt
Juice of 1 lemon
75g/3oz shelled frozen soy beans or green peas

> In a saucepan, boil the potatoes until tender, 20 to 25 minutes. When they are ready, drain and set aside.

> Preheat oven to 200°C/400°F/gas mark 6. Meanwhile, prepare the dough.

To make the dough:

> Pour the wet dough ingredients into a mixing bowl. Add 225g/8oz of the flour, and the turmeric, baking powder, and salt. Begin kneading the mixture, adding the rest of the flour gradually until a smooth not sticky dough is formed, about 10 minutes.

Set the dough aside, cover with a wet cloth or wrap in clingfilm, and begin preparing the filling.

To prepare the filling:

> In a large frying pan over medium heat, heat the oil, cumin seeds, and mustard seeds. The seeds will begin to pop. You may want to use a lid to keep from getting hit with any popping seeds. Let them pop for about a minute, then add the onions and carrots. Raise the heat to medium-high and sauté for 7 to 10 minutes, till the onions begin to brown. Add the garlic, ginger, coriander, turmeric, cayenne, salt, and lemon juice, and sauté a minute more. Add the potatoes, mashing the potatoes with the spatula or a potato masher as you go along. When potatoes are mashed well and heated through, add the soy beans and mix well.

> Divide the dough in half and on a floured surface roll the dough out thinly. Now comes the fun part (or, the pain in the ass depending on your temperament). Let's form the little cutie pies. Have a small bowl of water ready. With a 10cm/4in biscuit cutter (or something with a 10cm/4in circumference) cut out eight circles.

For small samosas:

> Cut the dough circles in half, creating semi-circles. Gently pull the dough to stretch it a bit. With your fingertips, brush the cut edge with water, then fold it over, corner to corner, and seal along the straight edge with your thumb and forefinger. You should now have a cone. Stuff 1¹/₂ to 2 teaspoons of filling into the cone, then dab the open edges with water and again seal with your fingers. Repeat until you have thirty-six samosas.

For larger samosas:

> Instead of slicing the dough circles in half, place 1¹/₂ tablespoons into the centre of an entire circle, then dab the circumference with water, fold over the filling to form a pillow-like semicircle, and seal with your thumb and forefinger.

To bake:

> Brush each side of the samosas lightly with oil and place on a baking sheet that has been sprayed with nonstick cooking spray or very lightly brushed with oil. For large samosas: Bake for 15 minutes. Flip the samosas over, bake for 10 more minutes, or until lightly browned. For small samosas: Bake for 12 minutes, flip over and bake for 8 minutes, or until lightly browned. I like to let them sit for at least 5 minutes, to let the crust flake just right. These freeze well; to reheat bake small ones at 180°C/350°F/gas mark 4 for 20 minutes, larger ones for 25 to 30 minutes.

COCONUT-MINT CHUTNEY

120ml/4fl oz coconut milk
5 tablespoons finely chopped fresh mint
5 tablespoons finely chopped fresh coriander
1 clove garlic, finely chopped
1 teaspoon pure maple syrup
1 teaspoon fresh lime juice
1/4 teaspoon salt

> Mix together all the ingredients in a medium-size bowl and refrigerate for 1 hour. Serve at room temperature.

···⟩ **PUNK POINTS**

To make frozen peas taste like peas and not like the freezer, run them under cool water to remove the icy freezer stuff, then drain.

MAKES 4 LARGE STUFFED PEPPERS

Again, this is a recipe inspired by my mom. She's been making stuffed peppers for years from a recipe off a veggie crumbles packet. She bugged me pretty much daily to put this recipe in the cookbook and I had to remind her, "Mom, no prepackaged foods, for the love of God!" One day she came over armed with the recipe and was determined to somehow force it into the cookbook. We came up with this recipe instead, and now everyone is happy.

2 tablespoons olive oil
1 medium-size onion, finely chopped
3 cloves garlic, finely chopped
150g/5oz mushrooms, finely chopped
1 tablespoon chilli powder
1 teaspoon salt
425g/15oz jar tomato sauce
3 tablespoons water
75g/3oz quinoa
4 large red peppers
400g can black beans, drained and rinsed
1 teaspoon pure maple syrup
Fresh coriander for garnish

> In a saucepan over medium heat, sauté the onions in the olive oil for 3 to 5 minutes, until the onions are translucent. Add the garlic and mushrooms; sauté about 5 minutes, until the mushrooms have released their moisture. Stir in the chilli powder and salt. Add the quinoa and 250ml/8fl oz of the tomato sauce (reserve the rest) and the water, lower the heat and cover, and simmer for about 20 minutes, stirring once.

> Meanwhile, preheat the oven to 180°C/350°F/gas mark 4 and prepare the peppers: Boil a pot of water. Cut the tops off the peppers and remove the seeds. Boil the peppers for 5 minutes and then drain them.

> Combine the beans and maple syrup with the cooked quinoa mixture. Stuff each pepper with filling and stand them upright in a baking dish. Pour the remaining tomato sauce over the peppers and bake for 15 minutes. Remove from oven, garnish with coriander, and serve.

MAKES 30 ROLLS

Crisp vegetables and sweet mango make the perfect treat for a hot summer's night, when the last thing you want to do is cook. The noodles are the only things that require cooking, and they're done in minutes.

1 mango, peeled and sliced into matchsticks
 (see Punk Points, page 153)
115g/4oz bean sprouts, or seedless cucumber, sliced into matchsticks
25g/1oz fresh coriander leaves
115g/4oz very thin rice noodles
4 tablespoons roasted peanuts, very finely chopped
20 rice paper wrappers (plus extra in case some tear)
Thai Dipping Sauce (recipe follows)

> Boil a medium-size pot of water. Turn off the heat and add the noodles. Let them soak for 10 minutes, stirring occasionally. Drain the noodles and run them under cold water until they feel cold. Transfer them to a bowl and begin your rolls.

> Fill a pie dish or large wide bowl with hot water (tap water is fine) and clean worksurface space or a chopping board. Place the rice paper wrappers, two at a time, into the water until they are flexible (30 seconds to a minute). Carefully remove from the water and lay flat on a clean surface. In the lower two-thirds of the roll, place a tablespoon of noodles and sprinkle a few of the chopped peanuts (about 1/2 teaspoon) over them. On top of that place five or six mango strips and on top of that place six or seven bean sprouts and three or four coriander leaves. Fold the left and right sides over the filling, then take the bottom of the wrapper and begin rolling. It may take a couple of tries to get it right, but keep it up and you're on your way to summer roll heaven. Keep wrapped and chilled until ready to eat and serve with small finger bowls of the dipping sauce.

THAI DIPPING SAUCE

MAKES 175ML/6FL OZ

3 tablespoons rice vinegar
3 tablespoons water
1 teaspoon Asian chilli oil
1 garlic clove, finely chopped
3 tablespoons roasted peanuts, chopped
1 1/2 teaspoons sugar

> Mix all the ingredients together and chill until ready to serve.

SEITAN AND HERB-STUFFED MUSHROOMS

MAKES 30 LARGE MUSHROOMS

These make great appetizers to an Italian meal. They are very omni-friendly so don't hesitate to serve them to anyone who still thinks passing you turkey at Christmas is funny.

40g/1¹/₂oz walnuts
30 large (about 5cm/2in in diameter) white mushrooms
  (about 675g/1¹/₂lb), wiped clean
115g/4oz seitan, diced as small as you can make it
3 tablespoons olive oil
1 small onion, very finely chopped
2 cloves garlic, finely chopped
¹/₄ teaspoon dried thyme
¹/₄ teaspoon dried basil
¹/₄ teaspoon dried oregano
¹/₂ teaspoon salt
Several dashes fresh black pepper
4 tablespoons chopped fresh parsley
1 teaspoon finely grated lemon zest
Juice of 1 lemon
40g/1¹/₂oz plain bread crumbs

> Preheat oven to 190°C/375°F/gas mark 5.

> Toast the walnuts: Heat a large frying pan over medium heat. Place the walnuts in the pan and toast for 3 minutes, turning frequently. Remove from heat and let cool. Chop coarsely and set aside.

> Remove the stems from the mushrooms. Set themaside. Place the mushrooms in a greased baking tin, stem side down, and bake for 10 minutes. Remove from oven. When cool drain off the liquid released by the mushrooms. While they are cooling, prepare the stuffing.

> Finely chop the mushroom stems. Heat a large frying pan over medium-high. Sauté the stems and seitan in the olive oil for about 5 minutes. Add the onion, garlic, dried herbs, and salt and pepper, and sauté for 5 more minutes. Add the parsley, lemon zest, and lemon juice, and mix well. Cook for 3 more minutes. In a large bowl, combine the vegetable mixture, bread crumbs, and toasted walnuts. Use your hands to mix well. If the mixture is too dry, add the reserved mushroom cooking liquid by the tablespoonful until the mixture holds together when pinched.

> Mound the filling into the mushroom caps, gently pressing it in. Bake filling side up in a baking tin for 20 minutes.

MAKES ABOUT 16 PANCAKES

The fresh, slightly sweet taste of parsnips doesn't need too much spicing up; the spring onions add just enough subtle bite.

500g/1¼lb peeled parsnips, grated
75g/3oz finely chopped spring onions
50g/2oz plain flour
2 teaspoons rapeseed oil plus extra for frying
½ teaspoon salt
A few dashes fresh black pepper
75-120ml/2½-4fl oz water

> Combine the parsnips and spring onions in a large mixing bowl, mixing to evenly distribute the spring onions. Add the flour, oil, salt, and pepper, tossing to coat. Add 75ml/2½fl oz water and mix until the batter holds together when given a squeeze. Add a little more water if necessary.

> Preheat a heavy-bottomed frying pan over medium-high heat. Add about 5mm/¼in oil. To test if the pan is ready, throw in a little pinch of the batter; if bubbles form around it immediately, it is ready. Form about 2 tablespoons of batter into a ball, then flatten out into a disc about 5cm/2in wide. Add the pancake to the oil, and continue with the rest of the batter, without crowding, cooking each pancake for 2½ to 3 minutes on each side, until golden brown. Note: I usually make a batch of eight, by the time the eighth is placed in the pan, the first pancake that I put in is ready to be flipped. You may need to add extra oil when you make the second batch.

PARSNIP-SPRING ONION PANCAKES

BLACK-EYED PEA AND QUINOA CROQUETTES WITH MUSHROOM SAUCE

MAKES 16 CROQUETTES

Quinoa is hands-down my favourite grain (even if it isn't technically a grain). Since it is a prerequisite for every vegetarian cookbook to tell you this, you probably know it is a complete protein. All too often it's made into a salad or thrown willy-nilly under a stir-fry. I wanted to give it the treatment in the form of these savoury croquettes. Serve with extra quinoa and Mushroom Sauce.

225g/8oz cooked black-eyed peas, drained,
    or 425g/15oz can, drained and rinsed
1 tablespoon olive oil
1 tablespoon soy sauce
175g/6oz cooked quinoa, at room temperature
1/2 teaspoon dried thyme, crumbled
1/2 teaspoon dried basil, crumbled
1 teaspoon paprika

For the bread crumb coating:
25g/1oz bread crumbs (I prefer whole wheat)
1/8 teaspoon salt
A few dashes fresh black pepper
1/2 teaspoon finely grated lemon zest
2 teaspoons olive oil

> Preheat the oven to 180°C/350°F/gas mark 4.

> In a mixing bowl mash the black-eyed peas with a potato masher and then with your hands. Add the olive oil and soy sauce and stir. Add the quinoa and spices and combine the mixture with your hands. You should be able to mould them into balls that readily stick together.

> In a small bowl mix together all the ingredients for the breading. Spray a baking tin with a little oil. Form the croquettes into walnut-sized balls. Gently roll the balls between your palms three or four times, then flatten out the ends so that the croquettes resemble marshmallows. Coat each ball with the bread crumbs and place on the prepared baking sheet. When all the croquettes have been formed, spray lightly with oil. Bake for 40 minutes, turning once after 20 minutes.

> I serve these by putting some cooked quinoa into the centre of the plate, then putting four croquettes around the quinoa, then putting a healthy dose of mushroom sauce on the quinoa. Don't pour the sauce directly on the croquettes or they will get mushy.

MUSHROOM SAUCE

This makes a great pasta sauce as well. To make it more of a gravy add 4 tablespoons of flour to the broth and arrowroot mixture.

750ml/22fl oz vegetable stock (page 76)
2 tablespoons arrowroot powder
1 tablespoon olive oil
1 small onion, finely chopped
2 cloves garlic, minced
115g/4 oz cremini mushrooms, thinly sliced
1 teaspoon dried thyme
1 teaspoon salt
A few dashes fresh black pepper
125ml/4fl oz white wine
3 tablespoons soy sauce
4 tablespoons nutritional yeast flakes
4 tablespoons plain soy milk

> In a small bowl whisk the arrowroot into vegetable stock until dissolved. Set aside.

> In a medium saucepan sauté the onion and garlic in the olive oil for 3 minutes. Add the mushrooms, thyme, salt and pepper and cook for 5 minutes, stirring occasionally. Add the white wine and turn the heat up high to bring to a boil for 3 minutes. Add the soy sauce and the broth/arrowroot mixture. Bring to a boil and then lower heat and simmer for 15 minutes, stirring occasionally. Add the nutritional yeast and whisk until dissolved. Add the soy milk and whisk for another minute or so. Let cool for a few minutes before serving.

FIZZLE SAYS

175g/6oz of quinoa contains more calcium than 1 litre of milk.

SPANAKOPITA (SPINACH PIES)

YIELD VARIES DEPENDING ON SHAPE (SEE BELOW)

My friend Terry brings us this awesome recipe that I have enjoyed at many a supper. She offers us three different ways to make it: a simple triangle shape, a wacky spiral, and a layered pie in a casserole dish. Sceptics take note: Terry's boyfriend is Greek so these pies have been under much scrutiny and they have passed the test.

6 tablespoons olive oil, plus extra oil for brushing the filo
2 bunches fresh spinach, rinsed very well, long stems removed
1 bunch spring onions, trimmed and finely chopped
3 cloves garlic, finely chopped
40g/1½oz chopped dill
900g/2lb firm tofu, drained and pressed
5 tablespoons fresh lemon juice
2 teaspoons dried oregano
Dash of ground or freshly grated nutmeg
75g/3oz finely ground walnuts
4 tablespoons nutritional yeast
1 teaspoon salt
Several dashes fresh ground black pepper
1 box frozen filo pastry, thawed overnight

> In a large heavy-bottomed pan warm 2 tablespoons of the olive oil over medium heat for a minute, then add the spinach, spring onions, garlic, and dill. Add the spinach in small batches if pan is too full. Sauté till completely wilted and soft and a good amount of liquid has sweated out of the greens. Remove from heat and set aside to cool to room temperature.

> In a large separate bowl mash the drained tofu (use your hands for more control) to a smooth but slightly grainy consistency. Take the cooled spinach mixture by small handfuls and squeeze out as much liquid as humanly possible (discard the liquid); add the squeezed spinach to the tofu. Add the lemon juice, oregano, nutmeg, ground walnuts, the remaining olive oil, and the nutritional yeast. Mix well with your hands, season with salt and pepper. Taste the mixture; it should taste pleasantly salty and tangy. Make sure the filling has cooled to room temperature before stuffing into the filo dough as directed below.

TRADITIONAL TRIANGLE SHAPE:

MAKES ABOUT THIRTY TRIANGLES

> Preheat oven to 180°C/350°F/gas mark 4. Take two sheets of dough; brushing olive oil generously onto one sheet, layer the second sheet on top, also brushing that sheet with oil. Score the stacked dough sheets lengthwise into three strips. With the short end of a strip nearest you, place a scant 2 tablespoons of filling toward the top left corner of the long rectangle. Grabbing the corner of the dough, fold it rightward so it forms a triangle, fold it toward the left to form another triangle, and continue folding in this manner till you just can't fold any more. Wrap any remaining bit of dough around, underneath the triangle. Brush with lots of olive oil and bake on a baking sheet for 10 to 12 minutes, till deep golden brown and puffy. These can burn easily, so watch it!

BACK-TO-ATHENS COIL SHAPE:

MAKES ABOUT FIFTEEN ROUND SPANAKOPITA

> Terry tells us: "I have no idea if Socrates would teach at the foot of a mountain of these back in ancient Greece . . . just that all the spanakopita I ate in Greece were shaped like these. They are basically cute snail-shaped buns. They never get as brown as the triangles and are a little less flaky but still yum."

> Preheat oven to 190°C/375°F/gas mark 5. Taking two sheets, brush with oil as for the triangles. Score the dough lengthwise into two strips. Run about 2 to 3 tablespoons of filling along one long edge of each piece. Carefully roll up the long strip, starting from the filling side, to form a long, thick rope o' spanakopita. Then, daintily roll up your coil to form a snail-shaped bun. Brush with lots of oil. Bake for about 25 minutes till golden brown on top and lightly browned on the bottom.

EASY AS P SHAPE:

SERVES 8

> You have no time for horrible Greek jokes so this one's for you: a spinach pie casserole, neat square slices well suited for serving a main course with salad.

> Preheat oven to 190°C/375°F/gas mark 5. Prepare eight sheets of dough with olive oil as for the triangle shape. Oil a 23 x 30cm/9 x 12in baking tin and place the dough layers inside, patting any extra dough up the sides of the pan. Gently spread the spinach mixture on top of the dough. Prepare another eight layers of filo (or add a few more layers if you have leftover dough), put on top of spinach layer, and tuck into the sides of the pan any overhanging dough.

> Lightly score the top layer of dough into 8 rectangles of equal size (this will prevent the dough from crumbling too much when slicing after it's baked). Brush with lots of olive oil. Bake 35 to 40 minutes till golden brown, being careful not to let the filo burn.

··✣ PUNK POINTS

> Filo is full of surprises the first time you handle it. You can't expose it to air for more than a few seconds before it dries out and becomes completely useless, so have handy several damp, clean tea towels and some clingfilm. It's easy once you get the hang of it, and you'll be making filo this and that all the time and soon your friends will have to plan some kind of intervention. To make your life easier, make sure you have plenty of workspace on a clean, smooth surface. Since you'll be working with olive oil, have handy one of those pump mist sprayers that you can fill with any oil of choice. Or just have a bowl filled with olive oil and apply with a pastry brush.

SERVES 6–8 AS A SIDE DISH

This is a nice healthy veggie-ful meal, especially if you're feeling lazy, since all the ingredients go into one pan. After the preparation work you bake it for an hour, while you kick back and pay the bills or update your blog. It is a little bland, but not in a bad way, since sometimes you just want the comforting taste of veggies without all those pesky spices. I would suggest making it this way once just to see that it is possible to make an eggless, cheeseless casserole and then doctor it with fresh herbs and spices some other time. I, however, love it just as is.

3 x 400g cans chickpeas, drained and rinsed
   (or equivalent amount cooked chickpeas)
1 large onion, quartered and thinly sliced
3 large carrots, grated
1 head broccoli, cut into small florets
2 tablespoons thinly sliced chives
25g/1oz bread crumbs (preferably whole wheat)
3 tablespoons olive oil
250ml/8fl oz vegetable stock
1 teaspoon salt

> Preheat oven to 180°C/350°F/gas mark 4.

> In a large bowl mash the chickpeas well, using a potato masher or a firm fork; it takes about 2 minutes to get the right consistency. Add the vegetables and mix well. Add the bread crumbs and mix, then add the oil and mix again. Finally, add the vegetable stock and salt, and mix one last time. Transfer all ingredients to a 23 x 33cm/ 9 x 13in (preferably glass or ceramic) casserole dish. Press the mixture firmly into the casserole. Cover with foil, bake for 45 minutes. Uncover and bake for 15 more minutes. Serve it hot on the day of cooking, but it tastes good cold as well.

CHICKPEA BROCCOLI CASSEROLE

CAULIFLOWER-LEEK KUGEL WITH ALMOND-HERB CRUST

SERVES 8–12

I was making this with my mom once and she kept exclaiming how wonderful the dill smells and how I should be grateful that the Absolute has provided such an abundance of fresh leafy things. Then she went on and on about how I should join her philosophy school so I could learn to appreciate things. Then she asked me why I don't get laser surgery to remove my tattoos. You see, in Jewish culture, even something as simple as a great-smelling herb can lead to nagging. Fortunately she only had yums and mmms while we were eating. This recipe was inspired by one in *Bon Appétit*, veganized, modified, and vastly improved.

2 medium-size heads cauliflower, cut into small florets
3 whole matzohs (unleavened bread available from Jewish delis)
350g/12oz silken tofu
4 tablespoons olive oil
2 leeks, coarsely chopped
1 small onion, cut into 1cm/^{1}/$_2$in dice
25g/1oz chopped fresh parsley
25g/1oz chopped fresh dill
1^1/$_2$ teaspoons salt
^{1}/$_2$ teaspoon ground black pepper
50g/2oz almonds, toasted and chopped

> Preheat oven to 180°C/350°F/gas mark 4.

> Boil a large pot of water. Add the cauliflower and cook for 10 minutes, covered. Meanwhile, prepare the matzoh mixture.

> Crumble the two sheets of matzoh into a food processor or blender. Grind the matzoh into crumbs; remove from food processor and set aside. Crumble the tofu into the food processor or blender, and purée until smooth. You may have to add a couple of tablespoons of water. Let the tofu sit until you're ready to use it.

> When the cauliflower is done, drain and transfer to a large bowl. Mash coarsely with a potato masher.

> Heat 2 tablespoons of the oil in a large frying pan over medium-high heat. Add the leeks and onions; sauté until the leeks are tender and the onions are translucent, about 5 minutes. Add to the cauliflower. Mix in the matzoh crumbs. Add the puréed tofu, 1 tablespoon of the parsley, 1 tablespoon of the dill, salt, and pepper, and mix well.

> Brush or spray a 23 x 33cm/9 x 13in casserole dish with oil. Spread the cauliflower mixture evenly in the dish. Mix together the almonds and remaining herbs. Crumble the remaining matzoh into large crumbs with your fingers and add the remaining 2 tablespoons of olive oil to them; mix. Sprinkle this mixture evenly over the kugel.

> Bake for 35 minutes, until browned on top. Remove from oven and let stand for 10 minutes.

FIZZLE SAYS

Kugel officially means "pudding" in Yiddish but in reality it describes any casserole.

YOUR KITCHEN WALL:

STRUCTURALLY IMPORTANT OBJECT HOLDING UP YOUR ROOF OR STORAGE FACILITY?

I am by no means an organized person. My brother-in-law likes to say I "don't believe in dresser drawers" because of the abundance of clothing on my bedroom floor. When it comes to my kitchen, however, I need things to be relatively organized or I know that it will only take that much longer to eat.

My method for organizing is basically this: Have as much hanging on the walls as possible. You can usually buy hanging devices relatively cheaply at most hardware stores, but if you aren't looking for anything fancy you can hammer some long nails into a long piece of strong wood and hang that up. I keep all of my pots, strainers, and most of my utensils on the wall, freeing up tons of valuable cabinet and shelf space. The other thing that's great about hanging pots and pans is that you won't fill up your draining board; you can simply hang them up to dry.

MAKES 16 PATTIES

One summer holiday, my fellow campers and I dressed up as falafel and sang a song to the tune of the Kinks "Come Dancing." Somehow I came out of all this still loving falafel to pieces. If you don't have a food processor, you can still make it by chopping the onions, garlic, and parsley as finely as possible and then mashing everything really, really, really well.

275g/10oz cooked chickpeas, drained, or canned chickpeas,
   drained and rinsed
15g/^{1}/$_2$oz whole wheat bread crumbs
2 tablespoons plain flour
1 medium-size onion, chopped
2 cloves garlic, chopped
^{1}/$_2$ teaspoon baking powder
1 teaspoon ground cumin
1 teaspoon ground coriander
^{1}/$_4$ teaspoon cayenne pepper
4 tablespoons chopped fresh flat-leaf parsley
^{1}/$_2$ teaspoon salt
A few dashes fresh black pepper
Vegetable oil for frying
4 large pita breads, sliced in half to make 2 pockets apiece
Lettuce
Chopped tomato, red onion, and cucumber
Tahini Dressing (page 121)

> In a food processor combine the chickpeas and bread crumbs; pulse for about 30 seconds until the chickpeas are chopped. Add the flour, onion, garlic, baking powder, cumin, coriander, cayenne, parsley, salt and pepper and process, scraping down the sides, until relatively smooth but somewhat coarse. The mixture should look fairly green from the parsley. Transfer to a bowl, cover, and refrigerate for at least ^{1}/$_2$ hour.

> Shape the batter into 4cm/1^1/$_2$in balls and then flatten into 5cm/2in diameter patties. In a large heavy-bottomed pan (cast iron is ideal) heat about 1cm/^{1}/$_2$in of vegetable oil. Test the oil by throwing in a pinch of the batter; if the oil immediately bubbles up rapidly, it is ready. Cook the patties in the oil in two batches, 2^1/$_2$ to 3 minutes per side. Remove with a slotted spoon and transfer to kitchen paper to drain.

> Prepare the sandwiches by stuffing the pita bread with falafel, lettuce, tomato, red onion, and cucumber, and drizzle with dressing.

FALAFEL

MAKES 4 SANDWICHES

I usually make a sandwich out of these but it would be just as good over a salad with a little citrus dressing. Mangoes and tempeh are surprisingly compatible and the curry powder pulls everything together.

225g/8oz tempeh
1 tablespoon soy sauce
1 small mango, peeled and chopped into 5mm/1/4in chunks
   (see Punk Points, page 153)
4 tablespoons spring onions, chopped

For the dressing:
3 tablespoons vegan mayonnaise
2 teaspoons curry powder
Juice of 2 limes
2 tablespoons cider vinegar
1 teaspoon sugar
1/2 teaspoon hot sauce
Pinch salt

For the sandwiches:
2 large pita breads, cut in half to make 2 pockets apiece
Thinly sliced red onion
Lettuce
Extra mango slices

> Tear the tempeh into bite-sized pieces and place in a small saucepan. Cover with water and add the soy sauce. Cover the pot and bring to a boil, then simmer for 15 minutes. Drain and transfer the tempeh to a bowl to cool.

> Meanwhile, whisk together all the ingredients for the dressing.

> Add the mangoes and spring onions to the tempeh. Add the dressing; mix well. Cover and refrigerate for at least an hour and up to overnight, to allow flavours to meld. Adjust the seasonings as you see fit. Serve in pitas with lettuce, red onion, and extra mango slices.

MAKES 6 BURGERS

Textured vegetable protein (TVP) gives these burgers a meaty satisfying bite, plus it ensures that the burger won't fall apart like so many homemade veggie burgers tend to do. Serve on buns with all your favourite toppings (I'm a mayo and pickles girl) and Sweet Potato Fries (page 114).

1 medium-size onion, finely chopped
1 small carrot, finely chopped
50g/2oz mushrooms, finely chopped
2 cloves garlic, finely chopped
2 tablespoons olive oil
350ml/12fl oz vegetable stock or water
3 tablespoons soy sauce
3 tablespoons tomato purée
150g/5oz textured vegetable protein
1/2 teaspoon dried thyme
1/2 teaspoon dried oregano
1/2 teaspoon dried paprika
2 teaspoons Dijon mustard
1 tablespoon peanut butter
1/4 teaspoon liquid smoke (optional)
4 tablespoons oat flour
Oil for cooking

> In a medium-size saucepan over moderate heat sauté the onion, carrot, mushrooms, and garlic in the olive oil for 7 minutes. Add the stock, soy sauce, tomato purée, vegetable protein, dried herbs, and paprika. Cover and bring to a boil, then lower heat and simmer about 7 minutes. Uncover and cook 3 to 5 minutes more, stirring occasionally, until the TVP is fully cooked and the texture is meaty.

> Transfer to a mixing bowl and let cool just until it is cool enough to handle (about 5 minutes). Add the mustard, peanut butter, and liquid smoke (if using); mix well. Add the oat flour and mix again. Cover and refrigerate for at least half an hour.

> Using about 3 tablespoons of the mix, roll into balls. Shape into burgers 6-7.5cm/21/2-3in wide. Preheat a large, preferably nonstick frying pan and pour in a very thin layer of oil (2 tablespoons should do it). When the oil is hot, add the veggie burgers and cook for about 5 minutes on each side; they should be nicely browned and firm to the touch. Serve with all your favourite burger toppings.

TEMPEH REUBEN

MAKES 4 SANDWICHES

If I haven't told you enough times, I was practically raised in a Jewish deli. I especially loved classic big Reubens sandwiches filled with plenty of sauerkraut, corned beef, Swiss cheese and Thousand Island dressing, and the non-traditional pickle. I do get a little misty eyed when I pass a deli and can't pay a visit to my lost love Reuben but sometimes he is waiting for me at home. I am not a big fan of soy cheese but if you are, feel free to add some grated Swiss-style cheese.

8 slices good, dark pumpernickel bread
8 teaspoons non-hydrogenated margarine
175g/6oz sauerkraut
2 dill pickles, thinly sliced
1 avocado, cut in half lengthwise and sliced into 5mm/¹/₄in slices
450g/1lb tempeh, cut into four equal pieces,
    then cut through the middle so that you have eight thin squares

For the marinade:
125ml/4fl oz white cooking wine
2 tablespoons olive oil
2 tablespoons balsamic vinegar
2 tablespoons tamari
2 tablespoons fresh lemon juice
2 cloves garlic, crushed

For the dressing:
5 tablespoons vegan mayonnaise
2 tablespoons ketchup
Juice of 1 lemon
1 tablespoon finely chopped onion
3 teaspoons capers
2 tablespoons sweet pickle relish (or equivalent amount chopped pickles)
A pinch of cayenne

Prepare the tempeh:

> Combine all the ingredients for the marinade. Add the tempeh and marinate for at least an hour, turning once.

> Mix together all the dressing ingredients and set aside.

> When the tempeh has marinated for an hour, preheat a ridged grill pan over high heat. Cook the slices on the grill for 4 minutes on one side, until dark grill lines have appeared, then use tongs to flip them over and cook on the other side for about 3 minutes.

Prepare the sandwich:

> Divide the margarine equally between the slices of bread and spread. Heat a large frying pan over moderate heat. Fry each piece of bread on the margarine side for 3 minutes, flip over and cook 1 minute more (it's OK that the other side is dry).

> Divide the sandwich ingredients equally among four margarine-side-down fried bread slices. Smother in dressing, top each serving with another slice of fried bread, plain side down, cut in half, and serve. For that authentic Jewish deli look, stick a cocktail stick in each half.

FIZZLE SAYS

You can get cans or jars of sauerkraut at the supermarket but for the best results ask a Jewish deli if they have any fresh sauerkraut.

TLT > TEMPEH, LETTUCE & TOMATO

MAKES 4 SANDWICHES

Tempeh, bacon, and hummus (and lettuce and tomato)—absolutely delish.

8 slices sourdough bread, toasted
1 batch Tempeh Bacon (page 31)
225g/8oz hummus
1 large tomato, thinly sliced
Thinly sliced red onion
4 leaves romaine lettuce
50g/2oz alfalfa sprouts

> Layer one slice of bread with hummus; pile on the tempeh bacon, then the tomato, onion, lettuce, and sprouts. Add a dollop of hummus to keep the sandwich intact, top with another slice of bread, slice in half, and serve. Repeat for the other three sandwiches.

MAKES 4 SANDWICHES

This combination of very simple ingredients produces a fresh-tasting salad that is perfect for those summer months when you just couldn't possibly cook.

450g/1lb extra-firm tofu, drained and pressed
3 tablespoons finely chopped red onion
3 tablespoons vegan mayonnaise
2 teaspoons Dijon mustard
2 tablespoons cider vinegar or fresh lemon juice
Salt and fresh black pepper to taste
8 slices whole wheat bread
Salad: lettuce, tomato, and onion

> In a large bowl, crumble the tofu with your hands for about 30 seconds, until you reach a crumbly but still somewhat firm consistency. Add the onion, mayo, mustard, vinegar or lemon and salt and pepper, chill for about 15 minutes. Serve on whole wheat bread spread with a little extra vegan mayonnaise and topped with lettuce, tomato, and onion.

TOFU DILL SALAD SANDWICHES

CHICKPEA-HIJIKI SALAD SANDWICHES

MAKES 4 SANDWICHES

OK you got me, I miss tuna fish sandwiches. These sandwiches satisfy my craving, and if you haven't cooked with hijiki before don't be intimidated — the taste is not incredibly fishy, especially in such a small quantity.

1 tablespoon dried hijiki
Boiling water
400g can chickpeas, drained
3 tablespoons vegan mayonnaise
2 tablespoons cider vinegar
2 tablespoons finely chopped onion
50g/2oz carrot, peeled and grated
Salt and fresh black pepper to taste
Salad: lettuce, tomato, and onion
8 slices whole wheat bread, toasted

> Place the hijiki in a small bowl and pour boiling water over it to cover. Cover the bowl with a plate and let the hijiki sit for about 15 minutes. Meanwhile, prepare the rest of the ingredients.

> In a large bowl mash the chickpeas with a potato masher until no whole beans are left. Add the remaining ingredients and mix well. When the hijiki is ready, drain and combine it with the chickpea mixture. Refrigerate for at least 15 minutes; serve on toasted whole wheat with lettuce, tomato, and onion.

FIZZLE SAYS

Hijiki, like other seaweeds, is a rich source of iron, protein, calcium, zinc, and iodine.

SIDE ORDERS

I ADMIT I DON'T GET TOO FUSSY WHEN IT COMES TO SIDE DISHES, SO ALL OF THESE RECIPES ARE FAIRLY SIMPLE. THE MOST VALUABLE THING ABOUT THIS CHAPTER, THOUGH, IS THE METHODS, BECAUSE ONCE YOU MASTER SEVERAL COOKING METHODS YOU CAN THROW AWAY ALL YOUR COOKBOOKS (EXCEPT THIS ONE) AND START A COOKING REVOLUTION. SO PREPARE TO ROAST, BAKE, BRAISE, AND BLANCH, AND WE'LL COOK A LITTLE RICE WHILE WE'RE AT IT.

SPICY INDIAN RICE WITH TOASTED ALMONDS

SERVES 6–8

I only do up my rice if I'm having friends over, otherwise plain basmati suits me just fine. But when I want to go the extra mile I make this to go with my curry. Frying the almonds intensifies the flavour and will have your guests wide eyed and asking what you did to the almonds to make them taste so good.

3 tablespoons vegetable oil
4 tablespoons slivered almonds
1 medium-size onion, cut into 5mm/$1/2$in dice
2 cloves garlic, finely chopped
1 small serrano chilli, seeded and finely chopped
   (or use jalapeño for less heat)
1 tablespoon finely chopped fresh ginger
2 teaspoons cumin seeds
$1/4$ teaspoon fennel seeds, crushed
2 cardamom pods
1 cinnamon stick
$1/2$ teaspoon salt
300g/11oz basmati rice, washed and drained
600ml/1 pint water
4 tablespoons raisins
1 carrot, grated

> Heat the oil in a heavy-bottomed pan over moderate heat until hot but not smoking. Cook the almonds, stirring frequently, until golden, about 2 minutes. Transfer with a slotted spoon to kitchen paper to drain.

> Add the onions to the pan and cook over medium-high heat for 5 to 7 minutes, until translucent. Add the garlic, chilli, ginger, spices, and salt and sauté 1 minute more. Lower heat and add the rice. Cook for 5 minutes, stirring frequently. Add the water, bring to a boil, then lower heat. Simmer uncovered for about 5 minutes. Add the raisins, cover, and cook over very low heat for 20 more minutes. When most of the liquid has been absorbed, turn the heat off. Add the grated carrots and almonds, mix well, cover, and let sit for 10 more minutes. When the rice is done, fluff with a fork and serve.

SERVES 6–8

This is an easy and tasty dish that looks pretty fancy with the toasted coconut on top. It's a perfect complement to BBQ Pomegranate Tofu (page 148) and it's also great with any Caribbean, Thai, or Indian dish.

400g/14oz jasmine rice, washed
400g can coconut milk
250ml/8fl oz water
1 cinnamon stick
1/4 teaspoon salt
Finely grated zest of 1 lime
40g/11/2oz unsweetened desiccated coconut

> Combine the rice, coconut milk, water, cinnamon stick, and salt in a saucepan and bring to a boil. Lower heat, cover pot, and simmer 20 minutes. Add the lime zest and stir with a fork. Remove from heat, cover, and let sit 10 more minutes.

> Meanwhile, prepare the desiccated coconut. Heat a frying pan over low-medium heat. Add the coconut and toast, turning frequently, for about 3 minutes, or until the coconut is browned and toasty.

> Remove the cinnamon stick from the rice and serve, sprinkling the toasted coconut over each serving. Garnish with lime wedges if you so desire.

COCONUT RICE WITH TOASTED COCONUT

SERVES 4–6

So easy, so good. I usually use thin-skinned potatoes but really any potato will work.

900g/2lb potatoes, cut into 2.5cm/1in chunks
3 tablespoons non-hydrogenated margarine
125ml/4fl oz unsweetened soy milk
1 teaspoon salt (or to taste)
Several dashes fresh black pepper

> Place the potatoes in a pan and cover with cold water. Cover and bring to a boil, then add some salt to the water. Re-cover and let boil for 20 minutes or so, until the potatoes are tender.

> Drain the potatoes, then add back to the pan. Add the margarine, and mash with a potato masher. Add the soy milk and mash some more until the potatoes are fluffy-ish. Add the salt, black pepper, and more soy milk or margarine if you think the potatoes need it.

···✣ **VARIATIONS**

> You can mix-and-match these flavour variations, if you like. For example, garlic-wasabi mashed potatoes are mighty yummy. Also, keep in mind that just about anything can be added to mashed potatoes: chives, curry powder, pesto... the possibilities are endless.

> **Garlic Mashed Potatoes:** Sauté 4 to 6 cloves of finely chopped garlic in 1½ tablespoons of olive oil and add to the potatoes when you add the margarine.

> **Wasabi Mashed Potatoes:** Dissolve 1 tablespoon of wasabi powder in the soy milk before you add it.

> **Spinach Mashed Potatoes:** Thaw a packet of frozen spinach and pat it dry, or chop a bunch of spinach and sauté in water only until wilted; pat the spinach dry with kitchen paper. Add to potatoes at the end. (Spinach and garlic mashed potatoes are especially good.)

PUNK ROCK CHICKPEA GRAVY

MAKES ABOUT 750ML/1¼ PINTS

I call this recipe "punk rock" because it depends on almost every spice in your spice rack; it would make any "real" chef gasp. But everyone knows that chickpeas are the punkest legume there is. It tastes so good, too, you'll make it at least once a week. I know it.

4 tablespoons plain flour
Approximately 600ml/1 pint water
1 tablespoon olive oil
1 medium-size onion, quartered and thinly sliced
2 teaspoons mustard seeds
3 cloves garlic, finely chopped
300g/11oz cooked chickpeas, drained, or 400g can, drained and rinsed
2 pinches of ground cumin
2 pinches of paprika
Pinch of dried rosemary
Pinch of dried thyme
Pinch of dried oregano
Pinch of ground coriander
3 tablespoons soy sauce
Juice of 1 lemon
4 tablespoons nutritional yeast

> Mix the flour with 475ml/16fl oz water until the flour is mostly dissolved.

> Heat a large frying pan (preferably cast iron) over medium heat. Add the olive oil and let heat for 20 seconds or so. Add the onions and mustard seeds; cook for about 10 minutes, stirring occasionally, until the onions are browned and the mustard seeds are toasted. Add the garlic and sauté for 2 minutes more. Add the chickpeas; use a potato masher to mash them—you don't want to mash them into a paste, just make sure each one is broken up although if there are a few whole ones left that is OK. Add the herbs and spices, soy sauce, and lemon juice. Scrape the bottom of the pan to loosen any browned bits of onion.

> Lower heat and pour the flour mixture into the pan. Stir constantly until a thick gravy forms. Stir in the nutritional yeast. If it looks too thick and pasty, add more water and mix well. It may look like it doesn't want any more water added to it, but just keep mixing and it will loosen up.

> Keep warm until ready to serve.

ANARCHA-FEMINIST POTLUCKS

In the late '90s I was feeling very isolated from any political community. I was working day and night to make ends meet. I even had three jobs: waitressing at two restaurants, and working at an organic produce warehouse. In my free time, I was either drinking or trying to write a novel that would never be finished.

I knew that I had to reconnect with my community—any progressive political community, really. My friend Amanda and I decided to start an anarcha-feminist potluck. The idea was this: every two weeks, get a bunch of hairy-legged women in a room together to share food, recipes, and politics. We would each bring a dish, eat, talk, and then have an informal roundtable where each woman would discuss where her political activism and interests lay. If you weren't politically active at the moment but wanted to be, you could say something like this: "My name is Eloise. I'm interested in prison reform work." Then someone, let's say Danielle, would say, "I'm active with Books Between Bars; let's talk after the meeting." And a prison reform activist would be born. We even had a little newsletter we passed out at meetings, called Eat Me, which listed events and happenings in the coming weeks. We also formed something called The Free(k) Economy, where each woman listed her skills, and whenever we needed help with something we could call on one another. It wasn't a barter system, rather a way for us to support one another in whatever way we were able to. I gave many haircuts and painted many rooms. Other women skill-shared: taught each other how to knit, weld, and even make homemade dildos!

Starting it was easy and this was before everyone and their Aunt Tilly had access to the Internet. We put up fliers in vegetarian restaurants, left-leaning bookstores, and colleges, and we also had a hotline number to call for information on the next potluck.

Some wonderful things came out of those potlucks, both culinary and politically. A lot of us helped to open a collective women's bookstore on the Lower East Side. We went to demonstrations together and hung anti-fascist fliers to telephone poles with wheat paste. And I'm not a big fan of street theatre, but I have to admit that some embarrassing street performances did occur. I like to think that sharing food in one another's home helped us to work together and trust each other in a way that sitting around in a sterile church basement with fluorescent lighting might not have.

SERVES 6

My best friend Erica is the kind of girl that throws a bunch of stuff together, pops it in the oven, forgets about it, goes to her sewing machine, makes a bag, remembers what's in the oven, takes it out, and it's delicious. These potatoes were always a hit at the potlucks, and when people asked for the recipe (and they always asked) she'd be like, "Potatoes, string beans, garlic, maple syrup, uhhhh, put it in the oven." Having lived with her for several years I was able to get hold of this recipe.

900g/2lb small potatoes, halved (about 2.5cm/1in pieces)
225g/8oz runner beans, halved, ends cut off and discarded
1 yellow onion, thickly sliced
2 cloves garlic, finely chopped
3 tablespoons tamari or soy sauce
3 tablespoons pure maple syrup
3 tablespoons Dijon mustard
2 tablespoons olive oil

> Preheat oven to 200°C/400°F/gas mark 6.

> Place the vegetables in a 23 x 33cm/9 x 13in casserole dish. In a mixing bowl stir together all the other ingredients until the mustard is dissolved. Pour over the vegetables and mix well until everything is coated. Cover with foil and place in oven. Bake for 25 minutes. Remove from oven and toss everything; use a spoon to drip the sauce over the veggies. Turn oven down to 180°C/350°F/gas mark 4, and cook for 25 minutes uncovered. Remove from oven, toss again, cook for 25 more minutes uncovered. These are especially yummy served at room temperature, with some of the remaining sauce poured over them.

MAPLE-MUSTARD-GLAZED POTATOES AND STRING BEANS

SWEET POTATO FRIES

SERVES 4

This was one of the first recipes submitted to my site by Beth and it got positive reviews all around. Reviewers suggested other spices, such as sage or chilli powder, so go ahead and be creative with your favourite spices. Even though sweet potatoes and yams are different, it is pretty common to use yams as you do sweet potatoes, so please don't get all technical on me; either one will work in this recipe.

2 large unpeeled sweet potatoes (about 900g/2lb),
   cleaned and cut into 5mm/1/4in strips lengthwise
1 tablespoon olive oil
1 teaspoon ground cumin
1 teaspoon ground coriander
1/4 teaspoon black pepper

> Preheat oven to 220°C/425°F/gas mark 7. Lightly grease a large baking tray.

> Combine oil, cumin, coriander, and pepper in a large mixing bowl. Add the potatoes and toss well to coat. Arrange in a single layer on the prepared baking tray. Bake for 15 minutes. Use tongs to flip potatoes over, and bake for another 10 to 15 minutes until browned.

SERVES 6

Nice spicy fries that are baked, not fried. These taste great with any sandwich, or by themselves when you're craving a savoury snack. OK, fine, I guess I don't need to tell you what to do with French fries.

4 large unpeeled potatoes, cleaned and cut lengthwise into
   10cm/4in strips
2 tablespoons olive oil
3/4 teaspoon paprika
1/2 teaspoon ground cumin
1/4 teaspoon dried oregano
1/4 teaspoon dried thyme
1/4 teaspoon cayenne
1/2 teaspoon coarse sea salt

> Preheat oven to 230°C/450°F/gas mark 8. Very lightly grease a large baking tray.

> In a mixing bowl toss the potatoes with the olive oil to coat. Mix the spices and salt together and toss with the potatoes to coat. It's OK if the mixture isn't coating every part of each potato; as long as there is some of the spice on each one, you're good.

> Arrange the potatoes in a single layer on the prepared baking tray; if they don't all fit use a second tray. Bake for 20 minutes. Use tongs to flip the potatoes, bake for another 12 to 15 minutes. The fries should be golden brown. Serve immediately.

BAKED CAJUN FRENCH FRIES

GINGER ROASTED WINTER VEGETABLES

MAKES 6–8 SERVINGS

Serve these sweet roasted veggies with garlicky greens and Grilled Tofu (page 147). They are beautiful to behold and the textures and flavours of the peppery parsnips, the sweetness of the squash, the gingeriness of the ginger, will send you into sensory overload.

450g/1lb parsnips (about 2 average-size), washed, peeled, and cut into 2cm/3/4in chunks
2 large carrots, washed, peeled and cut into 1cm/1/2in chunks
1 butternut squash, peeled, seeded and cut into 2cm/3/4in chunks
450g/1lb sweet potatoes (about 3 medium-size), peeled and cut into 2cm/3/4in chunks
2 heaped tablespoons grated fresh ginger
3 tablespoons pure maple syrup
5 tablespoons olive oil
Pinch cinnamon
Pinch allspice
1 teaspoon salt

> Preheat oven to 180°C/350°F/gas mark 4.

> In a large bowl combine all ingredients, making sure all veggies are well coated. Doing this with your hands works best.

> Place the veggies in a single layer on a baking tray. If they don't all fit you may need to use two baking trays and rotate them halfway through baking. If there is any extra liquid, pour it over the veggies.

> Bake for 25 minutes. Remove from oven and flip the veggies. Bake for 20 or so more minutes, until the veggies are tender inside.

SERVES 6

The sweetness of the beetroots is heightened with this simple, tangy orange glaze. Serve this with Roasted Vegetables (see preceding recipe), Grilled Tofu (page 147) and a grain. They're also really yummy if you chill and use them in a salad.

675g/1^1/$_2$lb beetroots (3 to 4 average-size), peeled, quartered,
   and sliced about 5mm/^{1}/$_4$in thick
250ml/8fl oz freshly squeezed orange juice
1 teaspoon finely grated orange zest
1 teaspoon pure maple syrup
1 teaspoon salt

> Place all the ingredients in a large pan, cover, and bring to a low boil. Simmer, stirring occasionally, for about 12-15 minutes, or until the beetroots are tender. Uncover and boil until the liquid has reduced to a glaze, about 4 minutes more. These taste good hot, at room temperature, or chilled.

ORANGE-GLAZED BEETROOTS

BRAISED CAULIFLOWER WITH THREE-SEED SAUCE

SERVES 4–6

Braising is basically sautéing and then steaming in its sauce, and cauliflower takes very well to it - it stays firm yet tender. This makes a nice side for any Indian-style meal; you can even make it a main course and serve over basmati rice or with Spicy Indian Rice (page 108) if you like.

2 x 400g cans tomatoes, in juice
1 large onion, finely chopped
3 tablespoons olive oil
3 cloves garlic, finely chopped
2 jalapeño chillies, stemmed, seeded and thinly sliced
1/4 teaspoon salt
2 teaspoons cumin seeds
2 teaspoons mustard seeds
1 teaspoon fennel seeds
1/2 teaspoon ground turmeric
1 bay leaf
1 head cauliflower, cut into large florets
1/2 teaspoon sugar

> Remove the tomatoes from their juice; scoop the seeds out of the tomatoes with your fingers. Chop the tomatoes into quarters and set aside. Reserve the juice from the can.

> In a large frying pan over medium heat, sauté the onion in the olive oil for 10 minutes. Add the garlic, jalapeños, salt, seeds and spices, and the bay leaf; sauté for a minute. Add the cauliflower and sauté for 2 minutes. Add the sugar and tomatoes and cook for a minute. Add 120ml/4fl oz of reserved tomato juice. Stir everything up, cover the pan, and let cook for 5 minutes, stirring occasionally. Uncover and cook for 5 more minutes, until the sauce thickens a bit and the cauliflower is tender but not mushy. Remove the bay leaf. This tastes best if you let it sit for about 15 minutes before serving.

SERVES 4

A splash of vinegar enhances these mushrooms to heavenly heights. Garlic adds punch. The beauty is in the simplicity. Be careful not to overcook.

3 medium-size portobello caps, sliced 5mm/¼in thick
1 tablespoon olive oil
3 tablespoons balsamic vinegar
Pinch salt
2 cloves garlic, finely chopped

> Preheat a large frying pan over medium-high heat for about 2 minutes.

> Toss the mushrooms with the olive oil until coated. Place in pan in a single layer. Let cook for 5 minutes, until they start releasing moisture. Turn over and cook another 2 minutes.

> Add the vinegar and salt; sauté for 30 seconds. Add the garlic and sauté for 3 more minutes. Tastes great warm, at room temperature, or chilled and used in a salad or sandwich.

···⊹ PUNK POINTS

> To get the garlic as thin as possible use a straight razor blade to slice it. Not only will you get really nice even slices but you will feel cool as hell doing it.

BALSAMIC-GLAZED PORTOBELLO MUSHROOMS

GARLICKY KALE WITH TAHINI DRESSING

SERVES 4

I love greens. You can prepare the kale without the dressing and serve it with... well, anything, really. I like to mash it into my mashed potatoes.

5 or 6 cloves garlic, thinly sliced (see Punk Points, page 119)
3 tablespoons olive oil
1 bunch kale, well rinsed and coarsely chopped
1/4 teaspoon salt
Tahini Dressing (recipe follows)
Lemon wedges to serve

> Sauté the garlic in olive oil over medium-high heat for about 2 minutes, stirring frequently, until golden brown. Add the kale and a few splashes of water. Use tongs to toss the kale around, coating it with the garlic and oil. Stir frequently for 4 to 5 minutes.

> Serve with a drizzle of Tahini Dressing. I like to use a squeezy bottle for this but if you don't have one just use a spoon. Garnish with lemon wedges.

FIZZLE SAYS

You can use the stems of the kale if they are on the thin side, about 5mm/1/2in wide. If they are larger, cut the leaves from the stem.

TAHINI DRESSING

MAKES 475ML/16FL OZ

This is way more than you need for the recipe above but I figure if you are making it you might as well have some left over for salad and sandwiches or falafel throughout the week. It is really important that you don't burn the garlic; you really just want to heat it and get the flavour into the oil.

8 teaspoons olive oil
3 cloves garlic, chopped
115g/4oz tahini
2 teaspoons balsamic vinegar
1/2 tsp salt
Juice of 1 lemon
Several dashes fresh black pepper
1/2 teaspoon paprika
120ml/4fl oz cold water
15g/1/2oz fresh parsley

> Heat the garlic in 6 teaspoons of the olive oil in a small sauté pan over very low heat for 2 minutes, just until it's fragrant.

> Place the heated garlic and all the other ingredients except the parsley in the food processor or blender, and blend until smooth. Add the parsley and pulse until the parsley is very finely chopped but not puréed.

> Refrigerate at least 1/2 hour in an airtight container. You may need to mix in a little extra water once it's chilled.

ROASTED APPLE SAUCE

MAKES ABOUT 1.2 LITRES/2 PINTS

This is a standard dish for me to serve as an alternative to that tiresome apple sauce from a jar. Serve it alongside potato pancakes or Horseradish and Coriander-Crusted Tofu (page 150) or any time you think, "This is good but it could use some apple sauce."

1.3kg/3lb dessert apples (about 10 apples)
Juice of 1 lemon
2 tablespoons rapeseed oil
3 tablespoons pure maple syrup
2 tablespoons sugar
1 teaspoon ground cinnamon
1/2 teaspoon finely grated lemon zest
Pinch ground allspice
1/4 teaspoon salt

> Preheat oven to 200°C/400°F/gas mark 6.

> Peel, core, and slice the apples into 2.5cm/1in chunks. Sprinkle with the lemon juice and set aside.

> Combine the oil, maple syrup, sugar, cinnamon, and zest in a glass baking dish, and whisk together. Add the apples and toss to coat.

> Roast until the apples are very tender, about 25 minutes, turning once after 15 minutes. Transfer to a large bowl and mash. If you prefer a smoother apple sauce, you can pulse it a few times in a blender or food processor. You can serve this warm, at room temperature, or chilled.

SERVES 4

Garlicky green beans and earthy mushrooms together at last. This is a great special occasion or as a side to any Italian meal.

1 tablespoon olive oil
3 cloves garlic, finely chopped
90g/3^{1}/$_{2}$oz cremini mushrooms, sliced
^{1}/$_{2}$ teaspoon dried oregano
4 teaspoons salt
A few dashes fresh black pepper
120ml/4fl oz vegetable stock or water
120ml/4fl oz white cooking wine
375g/13oz green beans, cut into 2.5cm/1in pieces

> In a large nonstick pan over medium heat sauté the garlic in the olive oil for about 2 minutes, stirring frequently. Add mushrooms, oregano, salt, and pepper, and sauté until the mushrooms begin to release moisture, about 2 minutes. Add the vegetable stock and turn the heat up a bit, bringing to a low boil. Simmer for about a minute.

> Add the white wine and green beans; cover and simmer for about 2 minutes. Uncover and cook for about 3 more minutes or until desired tenderness is reached.

SAUTÉED GREEN BEANS WITH MUSHROOMS

SESAME ASPARAGUS

SERVES 4–6

Serve alongside the Asian Grilled Tofu (page 146) or any Asian type meal.

2 cloves garlic, finely chopped
1 tablespoon toasted sesame oil
2 tablespoons soy sauce
2 tablespoons rice vinegar
1 teaspoon red chilli flakes
450g/1lb asparagus, ends discarded
2 tablespoons toasted sesame seeds

> Sauté the garlic in the sesame oil over medium heat for about a minute. Add the soy sauce, vinegar, and red chilli flakes. Add the asparagus and sauté for 4 to 5 minutes, until the asparagus is still bright green and firm but slightly tender. Move to a serving plate and sprinkle with sesame seeds.

SERVES 6

Believe me when I tell you that these are amazing. No, seriously. Roasting the Brussels sprouts gives them a popcorn-y flavour. Gone are the days of overboiled Brussels sprouts; this is seriously good food.

450g/1lb Brussels sprouts, washed and halved
1 tablespoon olive oil
3 cloves garlic, chopped
1/4 teaspoon coarse sea salt

> Preheat oven to 200°C/400°F/gas mark 6.

> Lay the Brussels sprouts on a baking tray; douse with the olive oil. Roast for 10 minutes. Remove from oven, add the chopped garlic, and sprinkle with coarse sea salt, using tongs and toss to coat. Return to oven, roast for 5 more minutes. Before you remove the Brussels sprouts from the pan, rub them into the garlic, and, when you serve them, sprinkle with whatever toasted garlic remains in the pan.

ROASTED BRUSSELS SPROUTS WITH TOASTED GARLIC

PIZZAS AND PASTAS

PIZZA IS THE MOST SOCIAL FOOD THERE IS. AS EACH PIZZA COMES OUT OF THE OVEN, ANTICIPATION BUILDS AS YOU WAIT FOR IT TO COOL JUST ENOUGH TO SLICE IT. THE CROWDS GATHER READY TO POUNCE AND FIGHT FOR THEIR SLICE IF NEED BE. AND THEN EVERYONE SITS AROUND EATING AND SAYING, "GREAT PIZZA!" AND COMING UP WITH TOPPING IDEAS FOR THE NEXT ONE. OR JUST LETTING YOU DO ALL THE WORK.
I PUT PASTAS HERE, TOO, TO HAVE A LITTLE ITALIAN CELEBRATION, AND BECAUSE THE PIZZA SAUCES CAN PERFORM DOUBLE DUTY AS PASTA SAUCES.

PIZZA DOUGH

MAKES TWO 35CM/14IN-DIAMETER PIZZA CRUSTS

250ml/8fl oz warm water
1¹/₂ tablespoons sugar
10g/¹/₄oz pack active dry yeast*
2 tablespoons olive oil, plus about 2 teaspoons for the rising bowl
350g/12oz plain flour
1 teaspoon salt
Cornmeal
* Not that rapid-rise stuff

> The first step is to prove your yeast. I've been told that with modern yeast this step is unnecessary, but my mother-in-law does it, so I will, too. Pour the water (warm, not hot) into a small bowl and dissolve the sugar in it, then add the yeast. Stir so the yeast gets wet, and let it sit in a warm place for 10 minutes or so. When you come back it should be foamy and maybe even bubbling a bit; if it is your yeast is alive. If nothing happened you'll have to start over with a new package of yeast.

> While you're waiting for your yeast to prove assemble the dry ingredients in a medium-size bowl. Once the yeast is ready, add the oil and the yeast mixture to the flour and salt and stir, or mix with your hands. You won't get very far before the dough balls up and doesn't want to absorb any more flour; don't worry, that's normal. Sprinkle a little flour on a clean worksurface and dump out the whole mixture onto it. It's time to knead.

> Kneading dough is more art than science; there's no right way to do it, as long as you get it mixed and stretched. Don't work it too hard; you're going to knead it for 10 minutes or so and you don't want to wear yourself out at the start.

> Your dough should be a little sticky; before you start, pat your hands with flour to keep them from sticking. If the dough is really, really sticky, work more flour into it as you knead. Soon the dough should become less sticky and easier to work, in a kind of magical way; now's the time to really start working it, stretching it out and squishing it with your hands. Don't be afraid to treat it rough; it likes it. The more you work it the stretchier and more elastic it will be, which is what you want.

> After about 10 minutes the dough should be nice and stretchy, still moist and tacky but not sticky or gooey. If it seems really tough and dry you've probably added too much flour. Don't worry; it happens.

You can still use it; maybe knead it a little longer and remember not to add as much flour next time. Pizza dough's not hard, but it takes a little practice to get it perfect.

> Form the dough into a ball. You'll need a clean bowl at least twice the size of your dough for it to rise in. Put in some oil (about 2 teaspoons) and then the dough, swirl it around a little, then flip it over. The idea is to get both the bowl and the dough covered with a thin film of oil. Cover the bowl with a clean, damp towel or clingfilm and set it in a warm place for about an hour.

> By then the dough should've doubled in size, more or less. Here's the fun part: uncover the dough and give it a firm punch so it deflates. Sprinkle some more flour onto your worksurface and dump the dough out onto it and start kneading. It should be stretchier and more pliable than it was before. Knead it for only about a minute, or until it's less like a sponge and more like dough again. Put it back in the bowl and cover it so it can rest.

> How long? It's up to you. You can freeze the dough now if you want and then defrost it and use it later. If you're impatient you can wait as little as ten minutes, but your dough won't be very stretchy. An hour or two is better. Either way, when you've waited long enough (and when your oven is hot enough; preheat to 240°C/475°F/gas mark 9 or as hot as you dare), sprinkle your worksurface with flour (again), take your dough out of the bowl, and cut it in two. Put one portion back into the bowl.

> Now it's time to stretch. Like kneading, stretching is an art and you'll get better with practice, so don't be discouraged if your first pizzas are uneven or small. Don't expect to be throwing it up in the air and catching it like they do in the pizzeria; those guys are pros. There's no right way; whatever works is good, but here's what I do: with my hands I flatten out the dough a little, and then I roll it out with a rolling pin until it's about 30cm/12in in diameter. Then I pick it up on one side and let gravity help me stretch it out; I work my way around it, trying to stretch it into an even circle, until I start to worry that it will tear. Then I sprinkle my pizza tray with a little cornmeal and set down the crust on it, pat it out a little bit more, and then apply the toppings. If the dough is just right and your stretching technique works, you should be able to get two 35cm/14in thin-crust pizzas from this recipe; but like I said, it takes practice, so if your pizzas are odd-shaped or lumpy, just say they're rustic.

> Now we're ready to make some pizzas!

PIZZA SAUCE

MAKES ENOUGH SAUCE FOR 4 PIZZAS

Pizza sauce is a simple thing, a little tomato sauce, a little garlic, a few herbs. It doesn't take much to create this most beloved sauce. The mistake some home cooks make is overseasoning it with all kinds of Italian spice mixes and whatnot—all it really needs is a subtle hint of the herbs.

2 teaspoons olive oil
2 cloves garlic, finely chopped
1 teaspoon dried oregano
$1/2$ teaspoon dried thyme
1 teaspoon salt
A few dashes fresh black pepper
600g/1lb 6oz can tomatoes in juice (plum tomatoes if you
   can find them)
2 tablespoons tomato purée

> In a saucepan over medium-low heat sauté the garlic in the olive oil for about 2 minutes, being careful not to burn the garlic. Add the herbs, salt, and pepper. Stir in the tomatoes, crushing them in your hand as you add them. Add about half the juice from the canned tomatoes, and the tomato purée. Increase the heat a bit and cook for about 10 minutes, stirring and crushing the tomatoes as you go. If the sauce looks too chunky, you can purée half of it in a blender (see Punk Points) and add it back to the rest of the sauce. Let cool to room temperature before using on pizzas. You can store whatever you don't use in the fridge for 3 or 4 days, or you can freeze it for up to 3 months.

···⟩ **PUNK POINTS**

> If you are using a blender to purée the sauce, let the sauce cool a bit so that the steam doesn't cause the blender lid to pop off and hot sauce to splatter everywhere. Once the sauce has cooled, give it a few pulses in the blender, lift the lid to let steam escape, and repeat.

MAKES TWO 35CM/14IN PIZZAS

Maybe you've noticed that my name sorta rhymes with pizza? I know someone else who realized that—everyone I've ever met EVER—from my kindergarten class on up. Well, it's finally come in handy! I can name a pizza after myself. Of course this pizza is awesome or it wouldn't be my namesake: salty olives, fragrant pesto, creamy tofu ricotta, and yummy cremini mushrooms.

Pizza dough for 2 pizzas (page 128)
Pizza Sauce (previous recipe)
Basil-Tofu Ricotta (recipe follows)
Classic Pesto (recipe follows)
5 tablespoons pitted and halved kalamata olives
25g/1oz cremini mushrooms, thinly sliced
Cornmeal for the pan
Olive oil for drizzling and brushing

> Preheat oven to 240°C/475°F/gas mark 9.

> Roll your dough out as described on page 129. Use the back of a big spoon to spread the pizza sauce onto the dough—use about 5 tablespoons or so—leaving about 4cm/1¹/₂in of space bare around the circumference. You should still be able to see some of the crust underneath—if you add too much it may make your dough soggy. Spoon the ricotta on, in mounds about 2 tablespoonfuls apiece—you'll want five mounds of it or so. Do the same with the pesto. You should have circles of pesto and ricotta but still be able to see the red sauce underneath.

> Scatter half the olives and mushrooms on top of the pizza. Drizzle a little olive oil on the mushrooms so that they don't dry out while cooking. Use a pastry brush to brush the crust around the circumference with a thin layer of olive oil.

> Place the pizza in the bottom of the oven on a pizza stone. Check it after 8 minutes. Once the crust is lightly browned your pizza is ready. It can take up to 12 minutes. Remove from oven and transfer to a large chopping board to slice. Proceed to your next pizza; by this point you should be feeling like a real pizza guy.

CLASSIC PESTO

MAKES 350ML/12FL OZ

"When in doubt—pesto" is my mantra. I serve it whenever I'm feeling lazy and want to cook something delicious that everyone will love. The nutritional yeast makes it creamier but it is entirely optional.

50g/2oz walnuts
130g/4^1/$_2$oz basil leaves
3 cloves garlic, smashed and coarsely chopped
1^1/$_2$ teaspoons coarse salt
125ml/4fl oz extra-virgin olive oil, or more to taste
4 tablespoons nutritional yeast (optional)
2 teaspoons lemon juice

> Place the walnuts on a baking sheet and toast them at 180°C/350°F/gas mark 4 for 10 minutes, turning once.

> Combine the walnuts, basil, garlic, and salt in a food processor or blender and process while you add the olive oil in a slow, steady stream. Add the nutritional yeast and lemon juice, and pulse to combine. The sauce should be the consistency of a slightly grainy paste, not a purée.

MAKES ABOUT 475ML/16FL OZ

Use as a filling for pasta shells, mixed with tomato sauce in pasta, or as a topping for pizza.

450g/1lb firm tofu, pressed
2 teaspoons lemon juice
1 clove garlic, finely chopped
1/4 teaspoon salt
Dash fresh black pepper
Handful fresh basil leaves, finely chopped (ten leaves or so)
2 teaspoons olive oil
4 tablespoons nutritional yeast

> In a large bowl, mush the tofu up with your hands, till it's crumbly.

> Add the lemon juice, garlic, salt, pepper, and basil. Mush with your hands again; this time you want it to get very mushy so squeeze through your fingers and mush until it reaches the consistency of ricotta cheese. This may take 2 to 5 minutes.

> Add the olive oil, stir with a fork. Add the nutritional yeast and mix all ingredients well. Use a fork now, because the oil will make it sticky. Cover and refrigerate until ready to use.

BASIL-TOFU RICOTTA

POTATO AND TEMPEH SAUSAGE PIZZA

MAKES ONE 35CM/14IN PIZZA

Potatoes on pizza? How zany. This was a popular topping choice on The Post Punk Kitchen message boards and I have to say, the boards are never wrong. Try to cut the potatoes as evenly as possible so that when they cook they are crispy outside and chewy inside. The fennel and tempeh are a match made in heaven, and the chewy potatoes make the marriage work. I love this pizza as is, but if you would like to add soy cheese I can't stop you.

Pizza Sauce (page 130)
115g/4oz grated mozzarella soy cheese (optional)
Tempeh Crumbles (page 30)
1 medium-size potato, scrubbed, cut in half and thinly sliced
  (slices should be under 5mm/1/4in thick)
1 medium-size fennel bulb, trimmed, very thinly sliced
4 cloves garlic, thinly sliced
Olive oil for drizzling and brushing

> Preheat oven to 240°C/475°F/gas mark 9.

> Roll out your dough as described on page 129. Use the back of a big spoon to spread the pizza sauce onto the dough—use about 75ml/ 2½fl oz or so—leaving about 4cm/1½ in of empty space around the circumference of the dough. You should still be able to see some of the crust underneath—if you add too much sauce, it may make your dough soggy.

> Sprinkle on the cheese, if using. Scatter half the other toppings randomly over the sauce, making sure that the potato slices and fennel lay flat for even cooking. Drizzle a little olive oil on the garlic, potatoes, and fennel so that they don't dry out while cooking. Use a pastry brush to brush the edge of the crust with a thin layer of olive oil.

> Place the crust in the bottom of the oven on a pizza stone. Check it after 8 minutes. Once the crust is lightly browned, your pizza is ready. It can take up to 12 minutes. Remove from oven and transfer to a large chopping board to slice. Proceed to your next pizza; by this point you should feel like you're an old hand at pizza making.

SOME PIZZA TIPS FROM A BROOKLYN GIRL WHO KNOWS PIZZA

> Don't overload your pizza with toppings, (a) because veggies contain water that will cook out as it heats, and this water can seep into your pizza dough and we don't want that; and (b) because the sauce and dough is delicious; it's nice to have an olive here and there, but if there's olives or mushrooms or what-have-you all over the thing it takes away from the pizza experience.

> Once your pizza dough is prepared keep it wrapped in clingfilm—it dries out fast! If it does dry out in some spots just do your best to rip off the dry parts and use the rest of it.

> You need a pizza stone for awesome crust. Sure, without one you may be able to get a serviceable crust—but for awesome crust a stone is a must. Its intense concentrated heat will ensure that you don't wind up with a soggy crust. If for some reason you refuse to buy a stone, place the pizza tray directly on the bottom of the oven in the last 2 to 3 minutes of cooking. If a pizza stone is too pricy you can use a "quarry tile" available at DIY shops; they only cost a couple of pounds.

> Experiment with textures and flavours. As long as you're not putting worn socks on the pizza it will probably taste good. I'm giving you a few of my favourite pizzas here but also try these toppings

> Roasted Red Peppers
> Roasted Brussels Sprouts (page 125)
> Pineapple and Tempeh Bacon (page 31)
> Artichoke Hearts
> Roasted Garlic (page 71)

GREEN GODDESS GARLIC PIZZA

MAKES ONE 35CM/14IN PIZZA

This is a beautiful pizza that is various shades of green and has a delicious roasted garlic base plus more garlic on top for good measure. It has a lot of components that are labour intensive but you will have the makings for dinner for the next two nights - use the remaining Garden Purée and pesto in pasta.

2 Pizza Crusts (page 128)
1 bunch spinach, well rinsed, leaves only
Salt
2 bulbs roasted garlic (page 71)
1 tablespoon olive oil plus extra for drizzling and brushing
Classic Pesto (page 132)
Garden Purée (recipe follows)
115g/4oz broccoli florets, chopped
50g/2oz pitted green olives
4 cloves garlic, thinly sliced
Cornmeal

> Preheat oven to 240°C/475°F/gas mark 9.

> Roll your dough out as described on page 129. Cover with clingfilm or kitchen paper until ready to use.

> Fill a frying pan with about 2.5cm/1in of water and bring to a boil. Add the spinach and sprinkle with salt; cook until spinach is wilted, about a minute. Drain in a colander and run some cold water over it; when cool enough to handle, press out as much water as you can. Set aside.

> Remove the roasted garlic cloves from their skins (just squeeze them and the garlic will come out). Place in a bowl and mash with a fork. Add a tablespoon of olive oil and mash into a paste.

> Spread half the garlic paste on the pizza dough. Spoon dollops of pesto on top, about 5cm/2in apart. Make 2 tablespoon mounds here and there of Garden Purée. Place half the wilted spinach, olives, broccoli florets, and sliced garlic randomly upon the pizza. Drizzle the vegetable toppings with a little olive oil to prevent their drying out. Brush the edge of the crust with olive oil.

> Place the crust in the bottom of the oven on a pizza stone. Check it after 8 minutes. Once the crust is lightly browned, your pizza is ready. It can take up to 12 minutes. Remove from oven and transfer to a large chopping board to slice. Proceed to your next pizza.

MAKES ABOUT 1.2 LITRES/2 PINTS

This is a fresh-tasting thick ricotta-like purée that is delicious as a lasagne or ravioli filling, or as a pasta or pizza topping.

450g/1lb asparagus, ends discarded, chopped into 7.5cm/3in lengths
450g/1lb green beans, halved, ends removed and discarded
115g/4oz frozen peas
115g/4oz slivered almonds
2 cloves garlic
40g/1¹/₂oz flat-leaf parsley
4 spring onions, green parts only, coarsely chopped
2 tablespoons extra-virgin olive oil
Juice of ¹/₂ lemon
¹/₈ teaspoon ground or grated fresh nutmeg
450g/1lb extra-firm tofu
40g/1¹/₂oz basil leaves, chopped

> Have ready a large bowl of iced water.

> Bring a large pot of salted water to boil. Add the asparagus and green beans; boil for 2 minutes. Add the frozen peas and boil for 2 more minutes. Drain vegetables and submerge in the ice water to stop cooking.

> Pulse the almonds into a fine powder. Add the boiled vegetables, garlic, parsley, spring onions, olive oil, lemon juice, and nutmeg; purée until smooth.

> In a large bowl, mash the tofu with your hands until it has a ricotta-like consistency. Add the purée and mix well. Fold in the basil. Cover and refrigerate until ready to use.

GREEN GARDEN PURÉE

HOMEMADE GNOCCHI

SERVES 6–8

There is no substitute, well, I should say, no good substitute for homemade pastas. Gnocchi are a nice place to start in your pasta-making journey because they are easy, delicious, and pretty difficult to mess up. If you are unfamiliar with gnocchi, they are a small, potato dumpling. There are a lot of accoutrements you can spend money on to give your gnocchi the perfect ridges that you find in the shop-bought or restaurant variety but I find that a long fork works just fine. This is my basic recipe to get you started but I've listed some of my favourite variations below. Make sure to try those as well! Serve with Classic Pesto (page 132), Sun-dried Tomato Pesto (page 179), or a simple tomato sauce.

900g/2lb potatoes, washed and scrubbed
2 tablespoons olive oil
1/2 teaspoon salt
175-200g/6-7oz plain flour

> Preheat oven to 200°C/400°F/gas mark 6.

> Poke four or five holes all over the potatoes. Bake them (you don't need a tray or foil, right on the oven shelf is fine) for 45 minutes to an hour, depending on the size. Do a test after 45 minutes; they should be very tender. Use tongs to remove them; place on a cooling rack and let them cool completely. This could take half an hour.

> Remove the skins from the cooled potatoes and place them in a large mixing bowl. Add the olive oil and salt and mash very well. You don't want to purée them, that will make the gnocchi sticky, just mash them until they have very few lumps. Add the flour in handfuls and incorporate it into the potatoes. Once you've added half the flour you can turn the dough onto a floured worksurface to work it there. Keep adding flour and lightly kneading the dough until a smooth, unsticky but not dry dough is formed.

> Divide the dough into thirds and roll each portion into a rope that is about 1cm/1/2in thick. Use a pizza wheel or a knife to cut the ropes into 2cm/3/4in long pieces. Now comes the fun part (well, I think it's fun)—flour your hands and use your thumb to roll each piece of gnocchi gently down the tines of a fork. Each piece should be able to do about half a roll before reaching the end of the fork so the final result should be that one side of the gnocchi has an indent from your thumb and one side has ridges from the fork.

> At this point you can sprinkle with flour and freeze any gnocchi you aren't using. To cook them immediately bring a large pot of water to a boil. Salt the water liberally and cook the gnocchi in three batches.

> Within 2 minutes they should rise to the surface; let them cook just under a minute longer and remove them with a slotted spoon. Transfer them to a large plate so that they aren't putting weight on each other and sauce them as soon as you can. I like them with either a simple tomato sauce or sautéed briefly with pesto and veggies.

⸱⸱⸳ VARIATIONS

> **Herbed Gnocchi:** After mashing the potatoes, add 2 tablespoons of chopped fresh herbs, such as oregano, thyme, and rosemary.

> **Sun-dried Tomato Gnocchi:** Use only 675g/1¹/₂lb of potatoes. Soak 115g/4oz of chopped sun-dried tomatoes in hot water. Cover and let sit until soft (10 to 15 minutes). Reserve about 3-4 tablespoons of the soaking water and drain away the rest. Purée the tomatoes in a blender or food processor until smooth, adding the soaking water by the tablespoon if needed to achieve a smooth purée. Add the tomatoes to the mashed potatoes. You may need to add 4 tablespoons or so more flour to the mixture.

> **Spinach Gnocchi: Finely** chop one bunch of well-rinsed spinach. Cook in a frying pan over medium heat in about 3-4 tablespoons of water until it is completely wilted. Place in a sieve and press all the water out. Add to the potatoes after they have been mashed.

FIZZLE SAYS

The best way to freeze gnocchi and not have them stick together is to line up the uncooked gnocchi on a chopping board or baking sheet (or anything big and flat) lined with parchment paper and sprinkled lightly with flour. Place the chopping board in the freezer for about an hour. Then you can transfer the gnocchi to freezer bags or lidded plastic containers and place back in the freezer for up to 3 months. When ready to cook, follow the directions in this recipe.

ORECCHIETTE WITH CHERRY TOMATOES AND KALAMATA TAPENADE

SERVES 2–4

Salty olives and tart, sweet cherry tomatoes taste luscious in this easy-to-prepare dish. I like to use orecchiette here because they cup the thick sauce nicely—but of course you can use whatever pasta you want to. This recipe is for 225g/8oz of pasta, which is supposedly four servings. If you are like most people I know, four servings = two servings, so plan accordingly. The tapenade recipe makes enough for 450g/1lb of pasta, though, so you can double the pasta and still have plenty of tapenade-y goodness to go around. If you have some left over, I suggest spreading it on toasted French bread for crostini or adding it to your sandwiches throughout the week.

225g/8oz orecchiette
1 tablespoon olive oil
1 medium-size red onion, sliced into thin half moons
450g/1lb cherry tomatoes, halved

For the tapenade
175g/6oz cups kalamata olives, pitted
3 tablespoons capers, drained
2 cloves garlic, chopped
Handful fresh parsley
1/2 teaspoon dried oregano
1/2 teaspoon dried tarragon
A few dashes fresh ground pepper
1 tablespoon red wine vinegar
2 tablespoons olive oil

Prepare the tapenade

> Combine all the tapenade ingredients in a blender or food processor.

Prepare everything else

> Prepare the pasta according to its package directions. While the pasta is boiling, sauté the onions and cherry tomatoes in the olive oil over medium heat for about 7 minutes.

> Reserve 125ml/4fl oz of cooking water from the pasta and drain the rest. Add the pasta to the tomatoes and sauté for a few seconds. Add 250ml/8fl oz of the tapenade and the reserved pasta water; stir to coat. When the tapenade is heated through it is ready to serve.

SERVES 4

This recipe is from friends who found a bag of pine nuts and they taught me to make this sauce, or something like it. I can't exactly duplicate the recipe because I think a lot of the flavour came from the fact that the pine nuts were "found." It's yummy to add some sautéed veggies on top of the pasta and some Grilled Tofu (page 147) wouldn't hurt either. Serve it with some home brew that may not have come out quite right. I guess it's like a vegan fettuccine Alfredo, but so so so much better.

225g/8oz fettuccine
2 teaspoons olive oil
1 medium-size onion, chopped into big chunks
4 cloves garlic, chopped
120ml/4fl oz water or vegetable stock
2 teaspoons English mustard
50g/2oz pine nuts, toasted (see Punk Points)
2 teaspoons soy sauce
2 teaspoons chilli powder
250ml/8fl oz nutritional yeast
1/2 teaspoon salt
A few dashes fresh black pepper

> Prepare pasta according to the directions on the packet.

> In a frying pan over moderate heat, sauté the onions in olive oil for 3 minutes, until just slightly softened. Add the garlic, sauté for 2 more minutes. Transfer to a blender, add all the other ingredients, and blend away. It should be somewhat smooth but still a bit grainy.

> This amount should be enough for four servings of pasta. You can reheat it in a saucepan over low heat if you need to. If you want to make it thicker, add more nutritional yeast by the tablespoon. To thin it out, add pasta water by the tablespoon.

> Drain the pasta and transfer it to a plate, spoon the sauce over the top, add veggies and tofu if using, and serve.

FIZZLE SAYS

To toast pine nuts, heat a heavy-bottomed frying pan over medium-high heat. Toss in the pine nuts and stir frequently for about 5 minutes, until they are lightly browned.

FETTUCCINE ALFREDA

THE MAIN ACT

I CAN NEVER ANSWER THE QUESTION
"WHAT IS YOUR FAVOURITE KIND OF FOOD?"
BECAUSE, WELL, "FAVOURITE" QUESTIONS
ARE SORT OF ARBITRARY AND THERE ARE
JUST TOO MANY ANSWERS TO CHOOSE
FROM. YET PEOPLE ALWAYS SEEM TO ASK.
MY STANDARD ANSWER IS "BROOKLYN
FOOD," BECAUSE IT SEEMS LIKE THERE
ISN'T ONE CULINARY PALATE THAT
DOMINATES MY BELOVED BOROUGH.
SO HERE YOU WILL FIND A DIVERSE
SELECTION OF DISHES INSPIRED BY EVERY
CORNER OF THE WORLD AND I NEVER HAD
TO LEAVE BROOKLYN FOR INSPIRATION.

TAMING YOUR TOFU

> Tofu is a delicious protein that can be quite versatile once you get the hang of using it. If you've been unsuccessful using it in the past, try these tips and I guarantee you will be a tofu pro in no time (well, in about the hour it takes to press it).

> The most important thing to know when dealing with tofu is that for a nice firm texture you will need to press all the water out. This will allow any marinade you soak it in to penetrate as much as possible, and will help it to crisp up when frying.

> Start with a drained block of extra firm tofu and place it between a clean tea towel or 3 or 4 pieces of kitchen paper on each side. Place a heavy, level object (like a hardback book) over the tofu. For good measure you can place another heavy object on top of the book. I often use a few cans of beans or sometimes a cast iron pan. Let it sit like that for half an hour, then flip it over for another half an hour.

> If you don't have a full hour to press the tofu, you can "quick press" it. Cut it into 4 even slices widthwise and press each slice very gently between your hands to get the water out. Then wrap each slice in kitchen paper and place under a heavy object as described above for as long as you can (at least 10 minutes).

> Freezing tofu creates a different, chewier texture. Freeze it in its packaging and let it thaw completely before pressing it. It's very important that the tofu thaws completely or else it will have a spongy unappealing texture. Frozen tofu tastes great crumbled into chillies and stews.

> Don't limit your tofu cuts to dices and thin rectangles. Below are some of my favourite ways to slice tofu. I find that different shapes and sizes can really up the visual aspects of any dish.

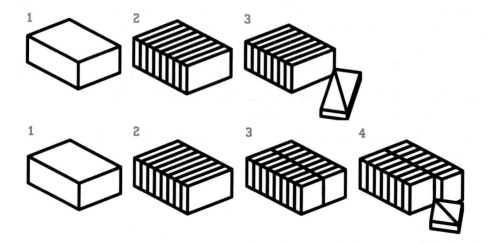

SERVES 4

This recipe calls for miso but it has a classic "meat and potatoes" taste and texture. It's a great meal to reheat the next day. I use chickpea miso for this dish but you can use whichever kind you like.

2 tablespoons arrowroot or cornflour
250ml/8fl oz vegetable stock
150g/5oz thinly sliced cremini mushrooms
4 tablespoons olive oil
1 large onion, quartered and thinly sliced
2 shallots, finely chopped
4 cloves garlic, coarsely chopped
1 teaspoon fresh thyme, chopped
Several dashes fresh black pepper
350ml/12fl oz white wine
1 tablespoon tamari or soy sauce
3 tablespoons chickpea miso
450g/1lb small potatoes, halved (or a larger potato cut into
   5mm/1/4in chunks)
450g/1lb tofu, pressed, cut into eighths widthwise,
   and then cut into two long isosceles triangles (see page 144)

> Mix the arrowroot with the vegetable stock to dissolve, and set aside.

> In a large frying pan sauté the mushrooms in 2 tablespoons of the olive oil over medium high heat for 5 to 7 minutes, until browned and most of the water has evaporated. Remove from pan and set aside.

> Sauté onions and shallots in the remaining 2 tablespoons of olive oil for 5 to 7 minutes until slightly browned; add the garlic, thyme, and black pepper, sauté for 2 more minutes. Stir in the white wine, arrowroot mixture, tamari, and miso. Bring to a boil, then lower heat to a simmer; the miso should be completely dissolved. Add the mushrooms, potatoes, and tofu. The pan will be crowded but make sure that all potatoes are mostly submerged in the gravy, it's OK if they stick out a little. Cover and simmer over low heat for 25 to 30 minutes, until the potatoes are very tender.

> Serve over mashed sweet potatoes or mashed potatoes or as a stew with some good crusty bread.

FIZZLE SAYS

Miso is prized for its many nutritional benefits; it is rich in trace minerals and dietary fibre.

STEWED TOFU AND POTATOES IN MISO GRAVY

MARINATED TOFU

I eat some version of the following recipes for dinner a few times a week because they are so easy yet produce amazing results. It's hard to remember that simple things can be extraordinary but these recipes prove just that. I've listed the marinade ingredients but the cooking methods are the same for both.

ITALIAN TOFU

SERVES 4 (OR 2, IF YOU'RE VERY HUNGRY)

450g/1lb extra-firm tofu, drained and pressed
125ml/4fl oz white wine
2 tablespoons olive oil
2 tablespoons balsamic vinegar
2 tablespoons tamari
2 tablespoons fresh lemon juice
2 cloves garlic, crushed
A big pinch each dried basil, marjoram, and thyme

ASIAN TOFU

SERVES 4 (OR 2 IF YOU'RE REALLY HUNGRY)

This tofu goes great with Wasabi Mashed Potatoes (page 110) and asparagus.

450g/1lb extra-firm tofu, drained and pressed
125ml/4fl oz mirin
3 tablespoons tamari
2 tablespoons rice wine vinegar
1 tablespoon sesame oil
2 teaspoons chilli sauce
2.5cm/1in piece fresh ginger, peeled and coarsely chopped
2 cloves garlic, smashed

Prepare the marinade

> Combine all marinade ingredients in a wide shallow bowl.

For grilled tofu

> Cut the tofu widthwise into four equal pieces. Marinate for an hour, flipping over after 30 minutes.

> Grease a ridged griddle pan (preferably cast iron) with vegetable oil. Preheat over a high heat for about 3 minutes. Use tongs to distribute the tofu slabs evenly into the pan. Gently use the tongs to press the tofu into the grill ridges, to get nice dark lines. Cook for 3 minutes on one side without lifting, then turn the slabs 90 degrees to create a crosshatched pattern on the bottom of the tofu. Cook for 2 minutes, then flip over and cook for another 2 minutes. Move to a chopping board and cut each piece diagonally across into two triangles with a sharp knife. (See illustration in "Taming Your Tofu, page 144.")

For baked tofu:

> Preheat oven to 200°C/400°F/gas mark 6.

> Cut the tofu widthwise into eight equal pieces. Marinate for an hour, flipping after 30 minutes.

> Place the tofu on a baking sheet and bake for 20 minutes. Flip over and bake another 10 minutes. Place under the grill for about 3 more minutes for extra chewiness.

⋯✦ PUNK POINTS

> Don't throw the tofu out with the bathwater; reserve your marinade and get creative. Remove the garlic and/or ginger and mix in a little water and arrowroot or cornflour, then heat it up and you've got yourself a gravy. Or, use it to stir-fry broccoli or asparagus for a nice, fast side dish: heat up some vegetable oil over high heat, then add your chopped vegetables, pouring on splashes of the marinade as you cook.

BBQ POMEGRANATE TOFU

SERVES 4 (8 IF YOU DOUBLE THE TOFU)

I love the floral taste of pomegranate and a little of the molasses goes a long way. I realize pomegranate molasses is an esoteric ingredient, but it's one of those things I was dying to try and it was well worth hunting out. I was even able to find it at the shabby grocery store around the corner from my apartment, but I think any well-stocked deli will have it; if not try a Middle Eastern grocery. You can double the tofu and still have enough sauce for the dish. I like to steam some veggies to go along with it and smother them in the extra sauce; served with the Coconut Rice (page 109) you've created something sublime.

For the tofu:
450g/1lb tofu, drained and pressed, sliced into eighths
2 tablespoons groundnut oil
1 tablespoon tamari

For the BBQ sauce:
1 tablespoon groundnut oil
3 shallots, finely chopped
2 cloves garlic, finely chopped
1/2 teaspoon Chinese five-spice powder
475ml/16fl oz vegetable stock
A couple dashes fresh black pepper
165g/6oz tomato purée
2 tablespoons smooth peanut butter
2 tablespoons pomegranate molasses
2 tablespoons tamari or soy sauce
3 tablespoons pure maple syrup
1 teaspoon hot sauce (or more to taste)
1 teaspoon liquid smoke

For garnish:
8 tablespoons pomegranate seeds

> Preheat oven to 180°C/350°F/gas mark 4. In a 23 x 33cm/9 x 13in (preferably glass or ceramic) baking tin, turn the tofu in the groundnut oil and tamari to coat on both sides. Bake for 15 minutes, then flip the slices and bake for 15 minutes more. Meanwhile, prepare the sauce.

> In a saucepan over medium heat, sauté the shallots in the groundnut oil for about 5 minutes, add the garlic and five-spice powder, and sauté 1 minute more. Add the stock and bring to a simmer. Add the rest of the ingredients (except for the pomegranate seeds) and bring to a boil. Lower heat and simmer for 15 to 20 minutes, stirring frequently.

> At this point, your tofu should be done baking. Smother the tofu with the BBQ sauce, return to oven, and bake 15 minutes more. Remove from oven. Serve with Coconut Rice and garnish with the pomegranate seeds.

FIZZLE SAYS

Pomegranates are delicious but a bit of a pain to eat. The only edible part of the grapefruit-size fruit is the outer casing of the seeds, which means you have to split open the fruit, take out the seeds, and remove the pits from the seeds to enjoy the sweet, tangy juice. They're very yummy, though, and if convenience is your thing you can buy pomegranate juice, pomegranate sauce, grenadine (made from pomegranates), and other stuff.

HORSERADISH AND CORIANDER-CRUSTED TOFU

SERVES 3–4

Most people are familiar with jars of horseradish, and that's all fair and well, but it's a whole other thing to experience this spicy root freshly grated. Briefly cooking the horseradish cuts down on the heat quite a bit, so don't worry that it will be too spicy for you. I serve this with a simple tartar sauce (2 parts vegan mayonnaise, 1 part sweet pickle relish) and Wasabi Mashed Potatoes (page 110).

For the marinade:
125ml/4fl oz white cooking wine
1 tablespoon tamari or soy sauce
Juice of 1 lemon
2 cloves garlic, crushed
450g/1lb extra-firm tofu, drained and pressed for at least an hour, sliced lengthwise into eighths

For the crust:
6 tablespoons panko (Japanese bread crumbs; if you can't find these, use unflavoured, preferably whole wheat bread crumbs)
6 tablespoons fresh mint, chopped
3 tablespoons grated fresh horseradish
Finely grated zest of 1 lemon
1 tablespoon coriander seeds, crushed (see page 28)
1/8 teaspoon salt
A few dashes fresh ground black pepper
1 tablespoon oil

Prepare the marinade

> Mix all ingredients together in a shallow bowl; marinate the tofu for at least 1 hour, turning occasionally.

Prepare the dish

> Preheat oven to 200°C/400°F/gas mark 6. Line a baking tin with foil and lightly coat in oil or spray with nonstick cooking spray.

> In a shallow bowl, mix together the bread crumbs, mint, horseradish, lemon zest, coriander, salt, and black pepper. Sprinkle with the olive oil and combine with a fork.

> Press each piece of tofu firmly into the mixture on both sides, one piece at a time. Take a small amount of the panko mixture and press it into the top side of the tofu (the underside will be less crusty because less crumbs stick to it; just a little sprinkle of crumbs should suffice on that side, otherwise too many will burn). Place each slice in the prepared pan.

> Bake for 15 minutes. Transfer to the grill for another 5 minutes. Serve.

FIZZLE SAYS

Once the horseradish is grated be prepared to use it immediately; it will develop a bitter taste if left around for too long.

MAKES 6 SERVINGS

The summer that I invented this mango tofu little could stop me from bringing it to any function that would have me. We had it grilled on the Fourth of July on a rooftop in Brooklyn while watching fireworks over the East River. The next week I brought it to a Leonard Cohen tribute concert. And then we enjoyed it again on my Mom's birthday. I started to get self-conscious that people might think it was the only thing I knew how to make, and they'd start calling me "Isa with the mango tofu," but really it's that good, you won't be able to stop yourself. Choose mangoes that are ripe but not overripe; they should give only slightly if you squeeze them.

For the marinade:
2 teaspoons groundnut oil
3 cloves garlic
4 tablespoons fresh ginger, coarsely chopped
1 jalapeño chilli, seeded and chopped
2 large mangoes, peeled and coarsely chopped
   (see Punk Points, page 153)
3 tablespoons pure maple syrup
250ml/8fl oz white wine or vegetable stock
2 tablespoons rice vinegar
   (use cider vinegar or red wine vinegar if you don't have rice)
Juice of 2 limes
250ml/8fl oz orange juice
1/4 teaspoon ground allspice
Fresh black pepper to taste
Dash of salt

For the tofu:
900g/2lb extra-firm tofu, drained and pressed cut into isosceles shapes
   (page 144)
1 mango, sliced into long, thin slices
1 red pepper, seeded and cut in long, thin slices

Make the marinade

> Preheat a medium-size saucepan over moderate heat; combine the oil, garlic, ginger, and jalapeño, and sauté for 7 minutes, being careful not to burn the garlic. Add the chopped mango and sauté for 5 more minutes.

> Add the maple syrup and wine, cover and simmer for 35 minutes. Uncover and simmer for 5 more minutes.

> Add the vinegar, lime juice, orange juice, allspice, black pepper, and salt; let cool, then transfer the mixture to blender and purée until smooth.

> Place the prepared tofu in the marinade in a sealable plastic bag or a tightly lidded plastic container. Marinate in the fridge for at least an hour and up to overnight.

Bake the tofu

> Preheat oven to 190°C/375°F/gas mark 5.

> Reserve about half of the marinade. Lay the marinated tofu in a single layer on a large baking tray or baking tin. Bake for 20 minutes. Flip over the tofu and add more marinade. Coat the peppers and remaining mango in the reserved marinade and add them to the pan. Bake another 15 minutes.

> Heat the remaining marinade in a saucepan and put in a bowl on the table (or floor, where ever you're eating) so guests can pour it over the tofu. Serve over jasmine rice with a steamed vegetable, such as asparagus or broccoli.

···⟩ PUNK POINTS

> There are several fancy ways to chop a mango but the way I usually do it is the most reliable (and of course the messiest). First, I peel it with a serrated peeler to prevent slipping. Then I place it on a chopping board, slice against the flat part of the pit, and then repeat on the other sides. Then simply chop the fruit slices as needed.

PUMPKIN SEED-CRUSTED TOFU

SERVES 3–4

Every year we buy a couple of pumpkins to cook with the best of intentions but they end up as decoration until they meet their demise. Well, not this year! This recipe utilizes the whole pumpkin—the pulp and the seeds. It's fun to pull together and it's got that homemade feel since you toast the seeds yourself. It's also really crunchy and flavourful, especially topped off with the cranberry relish. I hope this becomes an autumn tradition for you as it has for me.

1.3-1.6kg/3-3¹/₂lb pumpkin
2 teaspoons rapeseed oil plus extra for deep-frying
50g/2oz cornflour
4 tablespoons fresh oregano, chopped
¹/₄ teaspoon salt
450g/1lb extra-firm tofu, drained and pressed,
   sliced lengthwise into eighths
115g/4oz plain flour
250ml/8fl oz water

> Preheat oven to 150°C/300°F/gas mark 2.

> Carve out the top of the pumpkin with a paring knife and slice the pumpkin in half with a chef's knife. Remove the seeds and clean them in a sieve under running water (the holes should be big enough for the stringy bits to escape). Set the pumpkin aside to prepare as described below. Dry the seeds thoroughly by laying on a tea towel; pat the tops with another towel to remove any moisture. Measure 115g/4oz of seeds and transfer them to a baking tray. Sprinkle with 2 teaspoons of oil, toss to coat. Bake for 20 minutes, flipping occasionally. They should be toasted a golden brown to a deep golden brown. Transfer to a bowl to cool. Meanwhile, prepare the pumpkin.

> Adjust the oven temperature to 180°C/350°F/gas mark 4. Cut the pumpkin into slices that are about 5cm/2in wide at the widest point. Lightly oil the slices with oil. Place on a baking tray and bake for about 45 minutes, until tender and lightly browned.

> When the seeds have cooled, transfer them to a food processor and pulse until crumbly; the texture should range from ground to coarse and chunky. In a shallow bowl mix the seeds with the cornflour, oregano, and salt. Place the flour in another bowl, the water in another, and line up your three bowls: flour, water, and the seed mixture.

> Heat 5mm/¹/₄in oil over moderate heat in a heavy-bottomed frying pan, preferably cast iron. The heat should be between 160-180°C/325-350°F; if you don't have a thermometer test the oil by dropping a pinch of the seed mixture in; if bubbles form rapidly around the seeds, the oil is ready.

> Dip the tofu on both sides into the flour, then into the water, then into the seed mixture on both sides until the tofu is well coated with seeds. Repeat until all eight pieces are ready. Using tongs, lower the pieces into the oil (you may have to do it in two batches). Fry for 3 minutes on one side and about 2¹/₂ minutes on the second side. Remove from the oil and transfer to kitchen paper to drain the excess oil. Serve with roasted pumpkin.

CRANBERRY RELISH

225g/8oz fresh cranberries, coarsely chopped
125ml/4fl oz pure maple syrup
125ml/4fl oz water
3 tablespoons fresh orange juice
1 teaspoon finely grated orange zest

> Mix together all ingredients in a small saucepan. Cover and bring to a boil. Once boiling, uncover and let simmer for 15 minutes. Bring to room temperature and serve.

···⫶ PUNK POINTS

> When frying, the temperature of the oil is really important. Too hot and the food will burn; too cool and it won't cook properly. A frying thermometer is a pretty important accessory to have for this kinda stuff. If you don't have one, there are several methods to test if the oil is ready. One is to drop in some crumbs and see if bubbles form around it quickly; if the bubbles are out of control and smoky, it's too hot. If they are slow to form, the oil may need more heat or just a little more time. You can also use a wooden spoon: dunk in the handle and if bubbles quickly surround it, the oil is ready.

SEITAN

MAKES APPROX 1.3KG/3LB

In traditional seitan, the wheat flour is washed and kneaded three times over two days in order to develop the wheat gluten. I speed things up in this recipe by using vital wheat gluten flour. The flavouring for this goes well with pretty much anything, but depending on what you are using it for you can change the flavours a bit by adding finely chopped herbs. Or, if you're making something Asian or Indian, some grated ginger would be nice. The first time I made seitan I used a recipe from the book *Vegan Vittles*. This recipe was inspired by that one, but has been modified over the years to make it even more awesome.

225g/8oz vital wheat gluten flour
4 tablespoons nutritional yeast
2 tablespoons plain flour
250ml/8fl oz cold water or vegetable stock
125ml/4fl oz soy sauce
1 tablespoon tomato purée
1 tablespoon olive oil
2 cloves garlic, crushed or grated on a fine grater
1 teaspoon finely grated lemon zest

Stock
3 litres/5 pints water or vegetable stock
120ml/4fl oz soy sauce

> In a large bowl, mix together vital wheat gluten flour, nutritional yeast, and plain flour. In a separate bowl, mix together all the remaining ingredients for the seitan.

> Pour the wet mixture into the dry and combine with a firm spatula. Knead the dough for about 5 minutes until spongy and elastic. Let the dough rest for a couple of minutes. In the meantime, stir together the ingredients for the stock in a large pot (do not boil the stock at this point).

> Roll the dough into a log shape about 25cm/10in long and cut it into
6 pieces of roughly equal size. Place the pieces in the stock. It is important that the stock be very cold when you add the dough, which makes for a nicer texture and ensures that the seitan doesn't fall apart. Partially cover the pot (leave a little space for steam to escape) and bring the stock to a boil.

> When the stock has come to a boil, set the heat to low and gently simmer for an hour, turning the pieces every now and again.

> Turn off the heat and let the stock and seitan cool for at least 30 minutes. This will produce a firmer seitan. It is best to let everything cool completely before removing the seitan from the stock.

> What you do next depends on the recipe you are using. If storing the seitan for later use, slice it into bite-size chunks, put it into a sealable container, and cover with stock. Seal the container and place it in the fridge for up to five days.

JERK SEITAN

SERVES 4–6

This is the sort of recipe you can really play around with to your tastes. I rely on dried spices and storecupboard staples that are easy to substitute; the lime can be swapped with 3 tablespoons of cider vinegar, the maple syrup can be swapped with sugar. If you have a serrano chilli you can use that instead of or in addition to cayenne. This dish is pretty spicy as is, so taste the sauce before deciding that you want more heat.

For the marinade:
1/2 large white onion, coarsely chopped
2 cloves garlic, crushed
1 1/2 tablespoons chopped fresh ginger
3 tablespoons fresh lime juice
3 tablespoons soy sauce
2 tablespoons olive oil
2 tablespoons pure maple syrup
1 tablespoon dried thyme
1 teaspoon ground allspice
1/4 teaspoon ground cinnamon
1/4 teaspoon ground cayenne
1 teaspoon ground or freshly grated nutmeg

For the seitan:
450g/1lb seitan, cut into thick strips
2 teaspoons olive oil
1 onion, thickly sliced
1 green pepper, seeded and thickly sliced

> Prepare the marinade by puréeing all of the ingredients in a blender or food processor until relatively smooth. There will be some chunkiness but that's OK. Place the seitan in a shallow bowl and pour that marinade over it. Mix to coat. Cover and let marinate for an hour.

> In a large frying pan, sauté the onion and pepper in olive oil over medium-high heat for 5 to 7 minutes, until the onion starts to brown. Remove the seitan from the marinade and reserve the liquid. Sauté for 10 minutes, until the seitan has browned to your liking. Add the remaining marinade and cook for about 2 minutes to heat the sauce through.

> Serve with Coconut Rice (page 109), sautéed greens, and baked sweet potatoes or roasted autumn vegetables; ladle the extra sauce over each serving.

VEGANISM ON THE INTERNET

> The web can be a big scary place. A Google search for "vegan" will give you roughly three million results. If you don't already have a comfortable vegetarian home online,
or like my mom, you aren't web savvy, here are a few places I think you will enjoy.

⤐ COMMUNITIES

> **Veganporn.com** is the creation of Toronto-based vegan Herman Thrust. The first thing you notice when you go there is the surprising absence of porn, but he got your attention, right? This is a great site to keep up to date on current events—from genetic engineering to cat hunting in Wisconsin, Veganporn has got it covered. Members get their own journals in which to post their musings and Herman pulls from these journals, adding his commentary to make an informative and insightful and often humorous blog on the home page.

> **vegpeople.com** is such a great community. I don't know how they did it but it's full of intelligent, articulate, and well-informed people. I highly recommend it for the newbies in need of vegan support. Sections run the gamut from vegan fitness to book reviews, plus a section just for teens.

> **veganfitness.net** is a UK based community which deals with all sorts of issues that confront vegans. The forums discuss all aspects of vegan lifestyle with a strong focus on sports training and general health and fitness.

> **everythingvegan.co.uk** is a comprehensive vegan website with everything the vegan needs, from recipes and restaurant reviews to well informed forums and message boards. A must see is the animal ingredient list – essential reading for all vegans.
As the website says: 'If it's vegan it's here!'

> **veganfamily.com** is a website run by a vegan family in Scotland. The site covers all aspects of vegan lifestyle and all recipes and tips are tried and tested. Informative to anyone who wants to learn about veganism it also offers some great support for parents of vegan children.

> **veggies.org.uk/vbc.htm** The Vegan Business Connection lists all vegan businesses in the UK, including shops, restaurants, hotels and more. Ever wondered where to go for a vegan manicure, or where to pick up a vegan kebab? This is the site for you.

⋯⟩ BLOGS

> If you don't already know, blog is short for "web log." Cute, huh? There are millions of them and they can be fly-by-night. It's hard to sort the good from the bad, but here are a few that I check regularly.

> **vegblog.org** is Ryan MacMichael's account of his vegan journey. Well, it's not all so dramatic as that. Follow Ryan as he tackles recipes, reviews vegan products, discusses life as an animal rights activist, and provides analysis of vegetarianism in pop culture.

> **veganfreaks.org** is a relatively new site but became a fast favourite for me because our gregarious hosts Pleather and Vegannaise's posts are always so full of insight, information, and that darn critical thought that the kids love so much these days. A visit to Veganfreaks always leaves me thinking for at least a couple of minutes, and in Internet time minutes equal months.

> **whatdoveganseat.blogspot.com** is a 'growing catalogue of ordinary and extraordinary vegan foods'. As the blog is updated by several members there is a huge variety of recipes and all come with good quality photos and links to recipes.

⋯⟩ RECIPES

> Cooking with Chef Deb at **vegsource.com** (vegsource.com/talk/recipes/index.html) is an incredible message board where you can ask Chef Deb anything related to cooking and get an answer that day. Looking for a vegan trifle? Want to know the cooking time for Brussels sprouts? Chef Deb is the one to ask.

> PakuPaku (**pakupaku.info**) doesn't have a ton of recipes, but every single one is delicious and vegan, including a wonderful section of Ethiopian yumminess.

> **scentednectar.com/veg** is a huge website with links to hundreds of vegan recipes. The site covers such a broad range that it is bound to give you some ideas.

> **www.vegan-food-net** I like this site as it gives you the option to search for recipes by ingredient, great if you are wondering what to do with a few leftovers. Just type in what you've got in your fridge and it will give you tons of suggestions, easy!

SERVES 6

New York has some great Ethiopian restaurants and I make sure to stop in and eat with my hands whenever I'm travelling. Ethiopian food is usually served with injera (flatbread), but Savoury Crêpes (page 174) make an easy substitution or you can serve over rice.

For the purée:

6 serrano chillies, seeded and coarsely chopped
    (see Punk Points, page 65)
1 tablespoon chopped fresh ginger
2 cloves garlic, crushed
1 teaspoon ground cumin
1/4 teaspoon ground cardamom
1/4 teaspoon ground turmeric
1/4 teaspoon ground cloves
1/4 teaspoon ground cinnamon
120ml/4fl oz red wine
3 tablespoons olive oil

To prepare the seitan and peppers:

900g/2lb homemade seitan (page 156), cut into 5 x 1cm/2 x 1/2in strips
2 green peppers, seeded and cut into 2.5cm/1in strips

> Preheat oven to 200°C/400°F/gas mark 6.

> Place all the purée ingredients in a blender and purée until relatively smooth.

> Place the seitan strips and peppers in a 23 x 33cm/9 x 13in (preferably glass) baking dish; smother with the purée. Cover with foil and bake for 20 minutes. Remove the foil, flip the seitan and peppers, and cook for 20 more minutes. Serve with rice and vegetables.

SEITAN-PORTOBELLO STROGANOFF

SERVES 6–8

If you've been let down by vegan stroganoffs in the past let it go here and now; this dish will cure what ails you. The sauce has a rich "depth of flavour" and is bursting with creamy mushroomy goodness. I make my own seitan for this and I recommend that you do, too; it tastes better and is much, much less expensive. If you do make your own, then have it ready to be sautéed in the cast iron by the time you start the stroganoff. If you use shop-bought seitan you may want to use a little less than the 800g/1¾lb called for because it is so expensive. Supplement it with extra noodles and peas. This recipe makes a lot, so you may have plenty of yummy leftovers. Use it in a sandwich the next day!

2 tablespoons arrowroot powder (cornflour will work, too)
475ml/16fl oz cold water or vegetable stock
8 teaspoons olive oil
6 shallots, thinly sliced
1 large onion, quartered and sliced into half moons
3 cloves garlic, finely chopped
150g/5oz thinly sliced cremini mushrooms
2 portobello caps, thinly sliced
2 tablespoons fresh thyme, chopped
800g/1¾lb seitan, sliced into thin, wide strips
2 teaspoons salt
250ml/8fl oz red wine
1 tablespoon Hungarian paprika
8 tablespoons nutritional yeast
120ml/4fl oz plain soy milk
2 teaspoons Dijon mustard
115g/4oz frozen green peas
225g/8oz wide noodles, prepared according to the package directions

> Dissolve the arrowroot in the water; set aside.

> Heat 2 tablespoons of the olive oil in a frying pan over medium-high heat. Add the shallots and onions, sauté for 5 minutes. Add the garlic, cremini and portobello mushrooms, and thyme. Sauté for 15 minutes.

> Meanwhile, heat a cast iron frying pan with the remaining 2 teaspoons of olive oil, just long enough to coat it. Add the seitan and sauté over medium heat about 25 minutes, until it is dark brown and crispy on the outside. If you are using shop-bought seitan you need only cook it for 10 minutes.

> Back to the sauce: add the salt, wine, and paprika. Turn up heat to high to reduce the liquid, about 10 minutes.

> Lower heat to medium-high, add the arrowroot mixture, stir well, and let the sauce thicken, about 5 minutes. Add the nutritional yeast and mix well until it is dissolved. Add the soy milk and mustard and bring heat down to low; be very careful not to let it boil now because it can make the soy milk and mustard bitter. Add the seitan and peas; cook for 10 more minutes.

> Divide the noodles into bowls and mix with the stroganoff. It is best to mix immediately so that the pasta doesn't stick. You can top it off with tofu sour cream, but I like it just the way it is.

COLD UDON NOODLES WITH PEANUT SAUCE AND SEITAN

SERVES 4–6

Mmmm. I often get a dish like this on Allen Street on the Lower East Side at a vegan restaurant called Tien Garden. Temperature is important here to get the right taste sensations. The noodles and vegetables should be cold as can be, the sauce should be at room temperature, and the seitan should be warm. If you follow the directions you should have no problemo getting it all right. If you aren't serving immediately and the peanut sauce has been refrigerated, let the sauce sit out till it's at room temperature.

For the peanut sauce:
2 teaspoons groundnut oil
2 cloves finely chopped garlic
2 tablespoons finely chopped ginger
250ml/8fl oz water
2 tablespoons soy sauce
1 teaspoon ground coriander
150g/5oz smooth peanut butter
2 tablespoons pure maple syrup
3 tablespoons rice vinegar
2 teaspoons chilli sauce

For the seitan:
450g/1lb seitan sliced into 5mm/¼in strips
1 tablespoon groundnut oil
1 clove garlic
2 teaspoons soy sauce

To serve:
275g/10oz udon noodles
4 tablespoons black sesame seeds (optional)
1 seedless cucumber, halved across, sliced into matchsticks
250g/8oz mung bean sprouts
1 red pepper, thinly sliced
175g/6oz spring onions, chopped
Several lime wedges for serving

Make the peanut sauce

> In a small saucepan, sauté the garlic and ginger in groundnut oil over low-medium heat. Add the water, soy sauce, and coriander and bring to a boil. Add the peanut butter and turn the heat to low. Whisk well until the peanut butter and oil are combined. Mix in the maple syrup, vinegar, and chilli sauce. Remove from heat and let cool to room temperature.

Make the noodles

> Meanwhile, prepare your udon noodles according to the package directions. When noodles have cooked, drain them in a colander and rinse them under cold water until they are cool to the touch. Let them rest in the colander and prepare the seitan.

> Sauté the seitan slices in the groundnut oil for 5 minutes on each side or until the seitan is browned and yummy. Then sauté with the garlic for a minute, sprinkle with the soy sauce, and sauté again for 30 seconds or so.

> At this point, your peanut sauce should be at room temperature. Give the noodles a final rinse under cold water to make them cold and also to keep them from sticking together.

To serve

> To serve, place the noodles on a large platter. Pour the peanut sauce over the noodles, then sprinkle with sesame seeds. Scatter the cucumber, bean sprouts, and peppers on top, followed by the spring onions.
Place the warm seitan on top and place lime wedges around the circumference and gosh darn it you've got yourself a fine-looking meal.
If you would prefer to serve on individual plates to keep the greedy people from stealing all the seitan then just follow the directions dividing everything among four to six plates.

KABOCHA SQUASH STUFFED WITH BUTTERNUT VINDALOO

MAKES 6 STUFFED SQUASHES

Vindaloo is a spicy sweet-and-sour curry. Naturally sweet butternut squash tastes great in this and mellows out the spiciness. If you don't want to stuff the squashes you can just make the stew and serve over rice.

3 tablespoons groundnut oil
2 yellow onions, diced
3 cloves garlic, finely chopped
2 tablespoons grated ginger
1 tablespoon mustard seeds
1 tablespoon ground cumin
$1/2$ teaspoon ground cloves
4 cardamom pods
2 cinnamon sticks
3 tablespoons red wine vinegar
120ml/4fl oz red wine
400g can chopped tomatoes
675g/1$1/2$lb potatoes, peeled and cut into 1cm/$1/2$in chunks
675g/1$1/2$lb butternut squash, cut into 1cm/$1/2$in chunks
6 medium-size kabocha squashes
3 tablespoons pure maple syrup
Chopped fresh coriander to garnish

> In a stockpot over moderate heat, sauté the onions in oil for 5 to 7 minutes. Add the garlic and ginger; sauté until fragrant (about a minute); add all the seeds and spices and stir; add the red wine vinegar, red wine, and tomatoes. Mix to combine. Add the potatoes and butternut squash, cover, and bring to a low boil. Cook until potatoes are tender, about 25 minutes.

> Preheat oven to 190°C/375°F/gas mark 5. Lightly grease a baking tray. Cut off the top of the kabocha squashes and remove the seeds. Scrape inside with a tablespoon to remove the stringy parts. Cut a small sliver off the bottom of each squash so that the squash stands upright to stuff it. Place the squashes cut side down on the baking sheet, and bake for about 40 minutes. The squashes should be very soft and easily pierced with a fork.

> Back to the stew: When potatoes are tender, add the maple syrup and heat through. Cover and keep warm until the squashes are ready.

> Remove the squash from oven and, when cool enough to handle, stuff each with some of the stew. Garnish with coriander and serve.

START YOUR OWN PUBLIC ACCESS SHOW

> The Post Punk Kitchen is Brooklyn's fastest growing vegetarian punk rock cooking show because it's the only one. It is a "Bam!"-free space for vegetarians and food-lovers everywhere that came into being in 2003, born out of frustration over the garbage that the Food Network was trying to feed the masses (no pun intended). We believe that the airwaves and the risotto are for the people, not for corporations trying to peddle their processed-cheese wares. —**From the PPK mission statement**

> When I started doing The Post Punk Kitchen I had this idea that if everyone started their own shows then pretty soon we would fill the public airwaves with quality TV for the people.

> Public access varies from state to state but generally you pay a small fee to take a class that allows you to become a producer. The class should teach you very basic editing, filming, and lighting skills, but most importantly it allows you to use the station's equipment and facilities free of charge. With the help of other members you produce your show and you help them with theirs; eventually a star is born. It's such a great outlet for us little people to get our views and visions out there; take advantage of it. Start a radical gardening show, make a documentary about your pet snail, make a six-episode special about your grandma—the airwaves are ours!

CHICKPEA AND SPINACH CURRY

SERVES 6–8

I pretty much live on curries. I can't think of any other dish that packs so much flavour with so little work. I love tomato-based curries, and here the tomatoes are a pleasant backdrop and a sturdy base that isn't screaming tomato, so the spices can really shine through. It doesn't hurt that a tomato base has considerably less fat than, say, coconut milk, if you care about that sort of thing. Make sure your mustard seeds are visibly popping before adding the onions; if you've never cooked your own mustard seeds before, you are in for a treat that will change your curry making for good.

400g can whole tomatoes
3 tablespoons vegetable oil
2 teaspoons mustard seeds
1 large onion, cut into 5mm/$1/4$in dice
4 cloves garlic, finely chopped
2 tablespoons finely chopped fresh ginger
3 teaspoons curry powder
2 teaspoons ground cumin
1 teaspoon ground coriander
2 tablespoons finely chopped fresh ginger
$1/8$ teaspoon ground cloves
$1/2$ teaspoon ground cinnamon
$1/4$ teaspoon asafoetida (optional)
3 cardamom pods
1 teaspoon salt
450g/1lb fresh spinach, well rinsed and chopped
500g/1$1/4$lb chickpeas, cooked and drained,
　　or 2 x 400g cans, drained and rinsed

> Prepare the tomatoes by removing them one at a time from the can, squeezing out the juice, and tearing them into bite-size pieces. Place the prepared tomatoes in a bowl and reserve the juice in the can.

> Preheat a medium-size saucepan over moderate heat; pour in the vegetable oil and then the mustard seeds. Let the seeds pop for about a minute (you may want to cover the pot so that the seeds can't escape), then add the onion; turn up the heat to medium-high and sauté for 7 to 10 minutes, until the onion begins to brown. Add garlic and ginger, and sauté 2 more minutes. Add spices, salt and 3 tablespoons of the reserved tomato juice; sauté one minute more.

Add tomatoes and heat through. Add handfuls of spinach, mixing each addition until wilted. When all the spinach has completely wilted and the mixture is liquid-y, add the chickpeas. Lower the heat, cover, and simmer for 10 more minutes, stirring occasionally. Taste, and adjust the spices if necessary. Simmer uncovered for about 10 more minutes, or until a thick, stewlike consistency is achieved.

FIZZLE SAYS

Asafoetida is a root resin used in small doses in many Indian dishes. It's a little hard to find; so it is optional in this recipe. If you can find it though, you will fall in love with its aromatic scent and flavour.

SERVES 6

Making your own chilli paste is easy and flavourful. While admittedly you won't be saving money by not purchasing the chilli paste in a jar, you will embark on a culinary adventure that makes it worth it: the taste of homemade chilli paste is just incomparable. There are several steps here but you should be able to have dinner on the table within an hour provided your tofu is already pressed. This is a great dish to serve a date, alongside the Fresh Mango Summer Rolls (page 87) and some jasmine rice.

For the chilli paste:

2 small Thai green peppers or serrano chillies, seeded and chopped
2 jalapeño chillies, seeded and chopped
125ml/4fl oz boiling water
2 teaspoons crushed coriander seeds
1 teaspoon cumin seeds
5 white peppercorns (black peppercorns are an OK substitution)
1 tablespoon fresh chopped lemongrass (see Punk Points on page 171)
1 tablespoon chopped fresh ginger (or galangal if you can find it)
3 cloves garlic
40g/1½oz lightly packed fresh coriander, plus extra for garnish
2 teaspoons finely grated lime zest
6 shallots, chopped

Everything else:

5 tablespoons groundnut oil
1 block tofu, pressed and cut into small triangles (page 144)
1 red pepper, seeded and thinly sliced
1 medium-size red onion, sliced into thin half moons
400g can coconut milk
1½ tablespoons pure maple syrup
Juice of 1 lime
25g/1oz fresh basil (Thai basil if you can find it)

To make the chilli paste

> Place the serranos and jalapeños in a bowl, cover with about 120ml/4fl oz boiling water, and let sit for 15 minutes.

> Place the coriander seeds, cumin seeds, and peppercorns in a small frying pan and toast over medium heat for about 2 minutes, until they are fragrant. Transfer to a food processor and grind into a powder. (If you are using a blender instead, it may not grind the

seeds into a powder, it may just bounce them around, so either use a mortar and pestle or a coffee grinder to grind them or just place them with all the other ingredients and hope for the best.) Add the remaining ingredients, including the chillies in their water; grind to a paste. Cover and set aside until ready to use.

> Heat 2 tablespoons of the groundnut oil in a large nonstick frying pan over medium-high heat. Add the tofu triangles and heat on each side until golden brown (about 4 minutes per side). Transfer to a large plate and cover with foil to keep warm. In the same frying pan, sauté the red pepper and onions (add a little extra oil if needed) for about 3 minutes, until just slightly tender.

> Preheat a heavy-bottomed medium-size saucepan over low-medium heat. Add the chilli paste and cook for about 2 minutes, stirring constantly. Add the coconut milk and turn the heat up a bit. Mix together until the paste is incorporated; bring to a low boil. Add the maple syrup and lime juice, taste for sweetness, then add a little more maple syrup if necessary. Place the tofu, peppers, and onions in the sauce and cover; cook for 5 minutes. Add the basil and turn off the heat. Let sit for 5 minutes or so before serving. Transfer to serving bowls and garnish with fresh coriander.

⋯⋗ PUNK POINTS

Lemongrass looks sort of like a long stalk of bamboo but the only part you actually use is the heart of the stalk. You'll have to cut off the rest where the leaves start to branch and discard that, then peel off the rough outer leaves. The remaining "heart" can then be diced with a sharp knife.

SWEET POTATO CRÊPES WITH CORIANDER-TAMARIND SAUCE

SERVES 6

Terry and I made these for The Post Punk Kitchen's Valentine's Day episode (or rather, the anti-Valentine's Day episode) because they are sexy. The slightly sweet and aromatic filling wrapped in a warm chickpea crêpe and smothered in a rich yet delicate sauce is sure to impress. We toasted our own spices to bring extra-fresh flavour to the curried sweet potatoes, but if you don't want to go the extra mile, even though you really should, then you can use ground spices.

1 recipe crêpes (page 174)
2 teaspoons cumin seeds
1 teaspoon coriander seeds
1 teaspoon fenugreek seeds
1 teaspoon mustard seeds
2 cardamom pods
6 whole cloves
Pinch of ground cinnamon
Pinch of ground cayenne pepper
1/2 teaspoon salt

For the filling:
2 tablespoons groundnut oil
2 yellow onions, finely chopped
1 red pepper, finely chopped
2 cloves garlic, finely chopped
2 tablespoons grated ginger
1.2kg/2 1/2lb sweet potatoes,
    peeled and chopped into 1cm/1/2in chunks
1/2 x 400g can coconut milk
1 tablespoon pure maple syrup
1 tablespoon fresh lime juice

For the sauce:
50g/2oz raw cashews
75g/3oz fresh coriander
2 teaspoons tamarind concentrate
1/2 x 400g can coconut milk
1 teaspoon pure maple syrup
1 tablespoon groundnut oil
Pinch salt

To prepare the spice blend

> Heat a small frying pan over medium heat. Pour in all of the seeds, pods, and cloves except for the cinnamon and cayenne, and toast for about 3 minutes, shaking the frying pan back and forth for even heating. The spices should smell warm and toasty. Remove the mixture from the pan immediately and transfer to a bowl to cool. When fully cooled, place in a spice grinder (a coffee grinder works) or mortar and pestle. Grind to a fine powder and add the cinnamon, cayenne, and salt. Set aside.

To prepare the filling

> Preheat a large frying pan over moderate heat. Pour in the oil and heat, then add the onions and pepper, and sauté for about 5 minutes. Add the garlic and ginger; sauté about 2 minutes more. Add the spice blend and make sure the onions are coated with it. Add the sweet potatoes and cook for a minute or two. Cover the pan and cook for 15 more minutes, stirring frequently, until the sweet potatoes are tender. (You should prepare the sauce while they are cooking). Add the coconut milk, maple syrup, and lime juice, cover, and cook for 5 more minutes, stirring occasionally.
The coconut milk should be fully incorporated into the sweet potatoes.

To prepare the sauce

> Grind the cashews in a blender or food processor. Add the remaining ingredients and blend until smooth. That's it!

>There should be 2 crêpes per plate. Place one open crêpe on a plate, fill with about 6-8 tablespoons of filling and fold each side over, like a jacket. Repeat with a second crêpe and drizzle with tamarind sauce.

SAVOURY CRÊPES

MAKES 12 CRÊPES

This is Terry's recipe from when she worked in a vegan restaurant.
Don't worry if your first crêpe isn't perfect; even pros tear a crêpe or
two from time to time. Just move on to the next one.

175g/6oz all-purpose unbleached flour
50g/2oz chickpea flour
1 teaspoon salt
2 tablespoons olive oil
475ml/16fl oz water

> Combine the flours and salt in a medium-size mixing bowl. Make a
well in the centre of the flour and add the water and olive oil. Use an
electric hand mixer to blend until completely smooth (if you don't
have a mixer, mix with a fork for a good solid 3 minutes). Cover the
batter with clingfilm and let chill in the fridge for 1/2 hour or so.

> Preheat your crêpe pan or a nonstick frying pan that is 20cm/8in or
so across. Spray the pan with nonstick cooking spray or a very thin
layer of olive oil. Pour 3 tablespoons of batter into the pan; tilt and
rotate the pan so that the crêpe batter has covered the bottom and
crept up the sides of the pan just a tiny bit. When it looks like the top
of the crêpe has pretty much set and the corners of the crêpes are
just beginning to brown, flip over with a spatula and cook the other
side for just under a minute.

> You can remove the crêpe in one of two ways (and probably more
than two but this is how I do it: (1) fold the crêpe in half and then in
half again, so that it's folded into a triangular shape; or (2) use a
spatula to transfer the crêpe to a large plate, putting a sheet of
greaseproof paper between each crêpe to keep them from sticking.
You may be able to get away with not using the greaseproof paper if
you'd like to chance it. Either way you do it, cover the plate with foil
as you make the remainder of the crêpes.

SERVES 6–8

In Morocco a tagine is both a clay pot and the flavourful, aromatic stews cooked in them. This one is deliciously spiced, not authentic, but what the hell. It's full of vegetables and lentils, making it a powerhouse of nutrition. Serve on couscous.

2 tablespoons olive oil
2 medium onions, quartered and sliced thin
225g/8oz baby carrots, cut into 5mm/1/4in dice
1 serrano chilli, seeded and minced, to taste (see Punk Points, page 65)
3 cloves garlic, finely chopped
2 tablespoons grated fresh ginger
2 teaspoons ground cumin
1 teaspoon ground turmeric
1 teaspoon ground coriander
475ml/16fl oz vegetable stock
750ml/11/4 pints water
2 tablespoons tomato purée
2 cinnamon sticks
2 bay leaves
Several dashes fresh black pepper
225g/8oz dried red lentils, washed
1 courgette, halved lengthwise and sliced 5mm/1/4in thick
150g/5oz green beans, cut into 2.5cm/1in pieces
175g/6oz cherry tomatoes, halved
65g/21/2oz raisins
1 teaspoon salt
150g/5oz spinach, torn into pieces
15g/1/2 oz coriander leaves, chopped
15g/1/2 oz mint, chopped
Lemon wedges to serve

> In a stockpot, sauté the onions in the olive oil over medium heat for 3 minutes. Add carrots and chilli and sauté 3 minutes, garlic and ginger and sauté 2 minutes. Add the cumin, turmeric, and coriander, and mix. Add the stock, water, tomato purée , cinnamon sticks, bay leaves, black pepper, and lentils. Bring to a boil, lower heat and simmer, uncovered, for 20 minutes.

> Add the veggies (except the spinach) and raisins and salt, simmer 15 more minutes. Add the spinach, coriander, and mint; stir well. When the spinach has wilted completely (about 1 minute), turn the heat off. Let the stew sit for 10 minutes. Remove the bay leaves and cinnamon sticks. Serve over couscous with plenty of lemon wedges to squeeze in.

MOROCCAN TAGINE WITH SPRING VEGETABLES

BROOKLYN PAD THAI

SERVES 4

Is this authentic? Most assuredly not, but it does taste a lot like the pad Thai served all over in Brooklyn. When making pad Thai you have to make it only two servings at a time or the noodles will get mushy and the sauce won't be well distributed. This recipe is to serve four so you'll need to divide the ingredients between each cooking session. Once everything is prepared the actual cooking is only about 3 to 4 minutes, so everyone can still eat together. I use tongs to mix everything; they make it easier to not mush up the noodles.

450g/1lb rice noodles

For the sauce:
6 tablespoons tamari
6 tablespoons sugar
2 tablespoons tomato purée
2 tablespoons chilli sauce or hot sauce
3 tablespoons rice wine vinegar
3 tablespoons tamarind concentrate or lime juice

For the pad Thai:
6 tablespoons groundnut oil
450g/1lb tofu, drained and pressed cut into small triangles (page 144)
1 medium-size red onion, cut in half and thinly sliced
2 cloves garlic, finely chopped
1 tablespoon finely chopped lemongrass
125g/4oz bean sprouts
8 spring onions, sliced into 4cm/1¹/₂in lengths
2 small dried red chillies, crumbled
50g/2oz chopped roasted peanuts
4 tablespoons chopped fresh coriander
Lime wedges for serving

> Prepare the rice noodles according to the directions on the packet.

> Mix together the ingredients for the sauce.

> Preheat a large nonstick frying pan or wok over moderate-high heat. Pour 2 tablespoons of the groundnut oil into the pan and heat, then quickly add the tofu. Stir-fry for 4 to 5 minutes, until the tofu is crisp on the outside. Remove from pan and set aside.

> Pour 2 tablespoons more of the groundnut oil into the pan. Add half the red onion and stir-fry for 30 seconds. Add half the garlic and half the lemongrass, and stir-fry for 30 more seconds. Add half of the sauce and, when it starts to bubble (should bubble within a few seconds), add half the noodles. Cook for 2 minutes, stirring constantly, then add half the tofu, bean sprouts, spring onions, chillies, and peanuts. Stir for 30 more seconds. Transfer to two serving plates and garnish with coriander and lime wedges. Repeat with the remaining ingredients.

MILLET AND SPINACH POLENTA WITH SUN-DRIED TOMATO PESTO

SERVES 6–8

I got the idea for millet polenta from a fabulous book called *The Splendid Grain*. It's easier to prepare than polenta made with the traditional cornmeal because it doesn't require as much stirring and attention. This is a yummy version, flecked with spinach and oregano and topped with a savoury Sun-dried Tomato Pesto. Toasting the millet beforehand brings out its nutty flavour.

175g/6oz millet
750ml/1¼ pints vegetable stock
1 tablespoon olive oil plus more for cooking the polenta
75g/3oz shredded fresh spinach, well rinsed
1 tablespoon chopped fresh oregano
½ teaspoon salt
A few dashes fresh black pepper
Sun-dried Tomato Pesto (page 179)

> Toast the millet in a dry frying pan for about 5 minutes over high heat, stirring constantly until the millet releases a nutty aroma. Rinse in a fine-mesh sieve or a large bowl, until the water runs clear; drain as best you can.

> Bring the millet, vegetable stock, and olive oil to a boil in a saucepan. Lower heat and simmer for about 25 minutes. Mix in the spinach, oregano, salt, and pepper; simmer 10 more minutes, uncovered, until all the liquid is absorbed.

> You have a few options for moulding your polenta; it all depends on the shape that you want.

For squares or rectangles:

> Lightly grease a lidded plastic container that is roughly 28 x 18cm/11 x 7 in. Spread the polenta into the container and let cool on the worksurface. When fully cooled, cut into desired size rectangles.

For circles:

> Lightly grease two 400g cans. Spoon the polenta into the containers and pack tightly; let cool on the worksurface. When fully cooled, remove the polenta from the containers and cut into 2.5cm/1in slices. Note: It may take up to 2 hours for the polenta to get firm enough to cool in the cans. If you try to remove it before then, it will break and you will be sad. You may also need to drag a thin knife around the circumference to loosen the polenta.

Prepare the polenta:

> Preheat a large frying pan over moderate heat for a minute or two. Coat the pan with a very thin layer of olive oil; fry the polenta on each side for 3 minutes. Serve immediately, topped with Sun-dried Tomato Pesto, and with Roasted Asparagus on the side.

SUN-DRIED TOMATO PESTO

MAKES ABOUT 350ML/12FL OZ

This was submitted to my site by Frannie and I modified it a bit because I can't leave well enough alone. It's great as a pizza or pasta topping or on the Millet and Spinach Polenta.

115g/4oz sun-dried tomatoes
250ml/8fl oz water
4 tablespoons almonds
2 cloves garlic, chopped
2 tablespoons olive oil
1/4 teaspoon salt
A few dashes fresh black pepper
4 tablespoons fresh basil, chopped

> Place the sun-dried tomatoes in a saucepan and cover with water. Bring to a low boil, then turn the heat off and let soak for about 15 minutes, until soft.

> Grind the almonds in a blender or food processor. Add the sun-dried tomatoes (with the water), garlic, olive oil, salt, and pepper, and purée.

> Transfer to a bowl and stir in the basil. Let sit for a few minutes to allow the flavours to blend.

SPANISH OMELETTE

SERVES 6–8

This is another wonderful recipe from Terry, and even though it's an omelette it makes a great main course. She tells us, "If the anarchist revolutionaries in the Spanish Civil War had known about the magic of tofu they would have made a traditional dish just like this. Or maybe it's just my hopes for an egalitarian, non-authoritarian society talking again. Known in Spain simply as a 'tortilla' the thick, oven-baked omelette of eggs, potatoes, onions, and olive oil is found in virtually every café and can be eaten at any meal any time of day. Below is a liberatingly egg-free version—with the addition of saffron—that bakes to a beautiful golden yellow with the delicate flavour of the classic Spanish spice. The flavours improve with time so you can make it the night before and serve cold or at room temperature, along with a dollop of Roasted Red Pepper-Almond Sauce and crusty bread."

A small pinch saffron threads
3 tablespoons plain soy milk
4 tablespoons olive oil, plus extra for spraying omelette
1 medium-size onion, peeled, halved and thinly sliced
4 medium potatoes, unpeeled, halved and sliced into 5mm/¼in slices
    (make sure they're all the same thickness to ensure even cooking)
675g/1½lb soft tofu, drained
2 cloves garlic, crushed
1 teaspoon salt
Dash of cayenne pepper

> Place the saffron threads in a small cup and gently press the threads with the back of a spoon a few times; don't crush completely. Warm the soy milk in a small saucepan till just about boiling. Remove from heat and pour over the saffron; stir briefly and set aside for a minimum of 25 minutes. The longer the saffron soaks in the soy milk, the more flavour and colour will be released.

> Preheat oven to 190°C/375°F/gas mark 5. Pour 3 tablespoons of the olive oil into a 25cm/10in cast iron frying pan. Add the sliced potatoes and onions. The pan should not be completely full; there should be about 5mm/¼in of space left on top; remove some potatoes if it appears too full. Gently toss the onions and potatoes in oil to coat. Place in the oven and roast for 30 to 35 minutes, stirring on occasion, till onions are very soft and the potatoes are tender.

> Meanwhile, in a food processor blend till smooth the drained tofu, garlic, and remaining 1 tablespoon of olive oil. Strain the soy milk mixture with a fine-mesh sieve (if you're superthrifty you can save the saffron threads, dry them, and use once more) and add to tofu mixture along with salt and cayenne pepper. Blend till creamy.

> When the potatoes and onions are tender, remove from oven. Pour the tofu mixture into the pan and gently fold the potatoes and onions into the tofu mixture. With a rubber spatula, smooth the top, making sure to make the centre slightly more shallow than the outside; this will help ensure the centre cooks evenly.

> Spray the top of the omelette with olive oil and return to the oven. Bake for 50 minutes to 1 hour till the top is deep yellow and lightly browned in spots, and a knife inserted into the centre comes out clean. Remove from oven and allow to cool at least 20 minutes before cutting.

> To cut, run a knife along the edges, and press down on the omelette while slicing. To serve it real Spanish style you'll need to remove it whole from the pan: put a plate on top of the pan and with both hands securely holding pan and plate, flip the entire thing upside-down. Put on a worksurface and gently remove the pan—the finished omelette is oily enough so most of it should slide easily onto the plate. If you preferred the golden yellow side to be on top, simply flip again onto another plate.

> Excellent both warm and at room temperature. Serve as the Spanish do with ketchup (a good all-natural one worthy of revolutionaries) or with Roasted Red Pepper-Almond Sauce.

ROASTED RED PEPPER-ALMOND SAUCE

3 red peppers, roasted, skinned, seeds removed, and torn into chunks
4 tablespoons finely ground almonds
2 cloves garlic, peeled and crushed
3 tablespoons olive oil
3 tablespoons fresh squeezed lemon juice
1 teaspoon dried thyme
1 1/2 teaspoons sugar
Salt to taste

> Blend all the ingredients in a food processor until thick and creamy. Makes about 300ml/1/2 pint.

MUSHROOM AND SUN-DRIED TOMATO RISOTTO

SERVES 4

Risotto is a creamy rice dish that isn't difficult to make but does require a lot of maintenance; you need to stir it pretty much constantly. Try to get your roommates or family to help with the stirring, although when I make it alone I just blast some music and go into a Zen-like trance, where it's just the risotto and me on a hillside in Italy. I added truffle oil as an optional ingredient because it can be pricy, but you need only a few drops to add a deep, earthy mushroom flavour and that bottle can definitely last you a year or more; compared to the price of actual truffles that's quite a bargain.

1.5 litres/2^1/$_2$ pints vegetable stock
50g/2oz dried shiitake mushrooms
3 tablespoons olive oil
6 shallots, finely chopped
225g/8oz cremini mushrooms, thinly sliced
4 tablespoons chopped sun-dried tomatoes
2 garlic cloves, finely chopped
1 tablespoon finely chopped fresh thyme
2 teaspoons finely chopped fresh rosemary
^{1}/$_2$ teaspoon ground or freshly grated nutmeg
A few dashes fresh black pepper
^{1}/$_2$ teaspoon salt
300g/11oz arborio rice
A few drops black truffle oil (optional)

> Bring the stock to a simmer in a medium-size saucepan. Add the dried shiitake mushrooms and simmer for about 2 minutes, until the mushrooms are tender. Using a slotted spoon, transfer the mushrooms to a plate. When cool enough to handle, coarsely chop them. Cover the stock and keep warm over very low heat.

> In a medium-size saucepan over moderate heat, sauté the shallots for about 5 minutes; add the cremini mushrooms and sun-dried tomatoes, and cook until mushrooms are tender and most of the moisture has been released, about 7 minutes. Add the garlic, shiitakes, herbs, spices, and salt; sauté another 3 minutes.

> Add the rice and stir with a wooden spoon for 2 minutes. Add 250ml/8fl oz of stock; stirring often, simmer until the liquid is absorbed, about 6 minutes. Continue to cook and stir, gradually adding more stock, until the rice is tender and creamy and all the stock is absorbed. This should take about 30 minutes. Spoon onto plates and sprinkle some truffle oil over each serving if you like.

KNOW WHEN TO THRIFT

I have a thing against kitchen equipment that is shiny and new. I prefer the broken-in items that have been used and loved. Unfortunately, I found out the hard way that sometimes these things don't always love you back. In fact, they may electrocute you. My rule of thumb for buying used kitchen equipment is to avoid all things requiring electricity. Once an adorable waffle iron gave me the shock of my life and you would have thought I'd learned my lesson. But no, I just had to try a used blender, as well. It was from the '70s and the kind of avocado green that only existed in its pure form in that decade. The motor caught fire and the smoothie I was making flew hither and yon... it wasn't pretty.

My thrift-store utensils, however, have brought me much happiness. My handheld blender is unmatched in quality and design. I have a spatula that I use when cooking on cast iron. It is perfectly thin and wonderfully flexible, something I can't seem to find in shops nowadays. Spatulas are some of the kitchen products I totally recommend buying used. (If the fact that you don't know where something has been appalls you, just soak the item in a little bleach and put your worries out of your mind.) The kind of quality that was standard back in the day doesn't have to cost you today's prices. Of course, sometimes used items are called "vintage" and cost ten times as much as they should, so I usually avoid charity shops that are too conscious of their kitsch appeal.

AUBERGINE AND ARTICHOKE ALLA NAPOLETANA

MAKES AROUND 4 SERVINGS

This is bread crumb-coated aubergine layered with a Mediterranean artichoke "ragout" and smothered in Classic Pesto (page 132) and Sun-dried Tomato Pesto (page 179). You don't have to use artichokes; fresh courgettes makes a nice substitution. You need to use a lot of bowls and pans to make this, so don't say I didn't warn you. It's a tasty little dish, though, and worth all the fussing.

For the artichoke filling:
3 tablespoons extra-virgin olive oil
1 onion, finely chopped
2 garlic cloves, finely chopped
1/2 teaspoon dried thyme
1/2 teaspoon salt
A few dashes fresh black pepper
8 plum tomatoes, diced
350g/12oz coarsely chopped artichoke hearts
    (if using canned, be sure to wash off any seasoning)
50g/2oz thinly sliced, pitted kalamata olives
4 tablespoons capers, drained
4 tablespoons fresh basil, chopped

For the aubergine slices:
250ml/8fl oz water
1 tablespoon cornflour
115g/4oz plain flour
50g/2oz panko (Japanese bread crumbs; if you can't find these,
    use unflavoured, preferably whole wheat bread crumbs)
1/4 teaspoon dried thyme
1/4 teaspoon dried oregano
A few dashes fresh black pepper
1/2 teaspoon salt
1 large aubergine, sliced 5mm/1/4in thick
Oil for frying

Prepare the artichokes:

> In a large frying pan over medium heat sauté the onions in the oil until translucent—about 3 minutes. Add the garlic and cook 1 minute more. Add the thyme, salt, pepper, and tomatoes and cook until the tomatoes have broken down and released their juices, about 5 minutes. Add the artichoke hearts, olives, and capers; simmer for 10 minutes. Add the basil and cook 1 minute more. Cover to keep warm.

Prepare the aubergine:

> Have ready paper towel to drain the oil.

> In a wide bowl whisk the cornflour with the water until dissolved. Fill a dinner plate with the flour. Onto another plate sift together the bread crumbs, spices, salt, and pepper. Line up the dishes as follows: flour, cornflour mixture, panko.

> Heat a little over 5mm/¼in of oil in a heavy-bottomed frying pan over moderate heat. Dip an aubergine slice in the flour, then in the cornflour mixture, and then in the bread crumbs, flipping to coat. When you have dipped four slices use tongs to place them in the oil and cook until lightly browned, about 3 minutes. Flip over and cook 1 to 2 minutes more. Transfer to the paper to drain and proceed with the remaining aubergine slices.

Assemble the layers:

> Pour some of the sauce you are using onto the plate. Place an aubergine slice on the sauce, then a layer of the artichokes, then an aubergine slice, then another layer of the artichokes. Add one final aubergine slice and top with sauce.

···› **PUNK POINTS**

> Some say that sprinkling aubergines with salt removes the bitterness, although I am not convinced it is a wholly necessary step since some aubergines are specially grown to be less bitter. If you would like to try it for yourself, sprinkle the aubergine slices with salt and set on paper towel for half an hour. Rinse the salt off the aubergine, pat dry, and proceed with the recipe.

COOKIES AND BARS

I DEFY YOU TO SHOW ME ONE PERSON THAT DOESN'T LOVE A COOKIE. WHENEVER I WANT TO SAY THANK-YOU TO PEOPLE I BAKE THEM COOKIES, OR I AT LEAST THINK OF DOING IT. SOMETIMES I BAKE THE COOKIES AND JUST EAT THEM MYSELF AND THEN SEND AN E-MAIL WITH DANCING BUNNIES TO THANK THE PEOPLE INSTEAD.

SPARKLED GINGER COOKIES

MAKES 2 DOZEN COOKIES

Maybe these chewy, spicy sweet cookies are good any time of the year but I like to save them for the holidays. They make me nostalgic for the snowy winter days at grandma's cabin, sitting around the fireplace in our flannels singing... OK, fine, my grandma didn't have a cabin. There was no fireplace, no flannels, but these cookies sure make me wish there had been.

50g/2oz demerara sugar
225g/8oz plain flour
1 teaspoon bicarbonate of soda
1/4 teaspoon salt
2 1/2 teaspoons ground ginger
1/2 teaspoon ground cinnamon
1/2 teaspoon ground cloves
125ml/4fl oz rapeseed oil
3 tablespoons molasses
3 tablespoons soy milk
200g/7oz sugar
1 teaspoon vanilla extract

> Preheat oven to 180°C/350°F/gas mark 4. Lightly grease two baking sheets. Place the demerara sugar in a small bowl.

> Sift together the flour, bicarbonate of soda, salt, and spices. In a separate large mixing bowl, mix together the oil, molasses, soy milk, sugar, and vanilla. Pour the dry ingredients into the wet and combine well. Roll into 2.5cm/1in balls, flatten into a 4cm/1 1/2in diameter disc, press the cookie tops into the demerara sugar and place 2.5cm/1in apart sugar side up on a prepared baking sheet. Bake 10 to 12 minutes, let cool on baking sheets for 3 to 5 minutes, transfer to cooling rack.

MAKES 3 DOZEN COOKIES

There's nothing healthy about these. I feel like I have to get that out of the way because sometimes people think vegan translates into healthy and although I usually try to make my cookies a little bit more healthy than your average cookie, I didn't even bother here. This cookie was made for the sole purpose of proving to someone I work with that my vegan cookies were just as good as his unvegan ones, and it worked!

225g/8oz non-hydrogenated margarine, at room temperature
250g/9oz sugar
1 tablespoon molasses
2 teaspoons vanilla extract
500g/1¼lb plain flour
1 teaspoon bicarbonate of soda
1 teaspoon salt
200g/7oz plain chocolate chips

> Preheat oven to 180°C/350°F/gas mark 4.

> Cream together the margarine and sugar until fluffy. Add the molasses and vanilla. Add the flour, bicarbonate of soda, and salt, and mix well. Fold in the chocolate chips. Drop by teaspoonfuls spaced a little over 5cm/2in apart onto ungreased baking sheets. Bake for 8 to 10 minutes, until ever so slightly browned. Let cool on the baking sheets for 5 minutes, then transfer to a cooling rack.

CHOCOLATE
CHIP COOKIES

MAPLE WALNUT COOKIES

MAKES 3 DOZEN COOKIES

When I first discovered maple extract you couldn't stop me from adding it to everything. These are buttery, chewy, and rich – perfect for a cool autumn day with a warming drink.

125ml/4fl oz rapeseed oil
3 tablespoons pure maple syrup
2 tablespoons molasses
1 teaspoon vanilla extract
2 teaspoons maple extract
150g/5oz sugar
3 tablespoons rice or soy milk
2 tablespoons tapioca starch, arrowroot or cornflour
175g/6oz plain flour
3/4 teaspoon salt
1 teaspoon bicarbonate of soda
175g/6oz chopped walnuts
3 dozen walnut halves

> Preheat oven to 180°C/350°F/gas mark 4. Lightly grease three baking sheets or line them with parchment paper.

> Combine the oil, maple syrup, molasses, vanilla and maple extracts, and sugar in a mixing bowl and stir until well combined. The oil will separate a little but that's OK. Add the soy milk and tapioca starch and mix until the tapioca is dissolved and the mixture resembles caramel.

> Add the flour, salt, and bicarbonate of soda. Mix with a wooden spoon until well combined. Fold in the chopped walnuts.

> Drop by tablespoonfuls about 5cm/2in apart onto the prepared baking sheets. Press a walnut half into the centre of each cookie. Bake for 8 to 10 minutes. Remove from oven, let sit for 2 minutes, then transfer to a cooling rack.

VEGANIZE IT!

⋯⊹ GET RID OF THE EGGS

Replacing eggs is the most challenging aspect of vegan baking. Those suckers bind, they leaven, and they give structure to our baked goods. However, like a bad boyfriend, they can be replaced, and with pleasing results. Here's some info on replacements I have tried.

⋯⊹ FLAX SEEDS

How to use:

1 tablespoon flax seeds plus 3 tablespoons water replaces one egg. Finely grind 1 tablespoon whole flax seeds in a blender or coffee grinder, or use 2 tablespoons pre-ground flax seeds. Transfer to a bowl and beat in 3 tablespoons of water using a whisk or fork. It will become very gooey and gelatinous, much like an egg white. In some recipes, you can leave the ground flax seeds in the blender and add the other wet ingredients to it, thus saving you the extra step of the bowl.

When it works best:

Flax seeds have a distinct earthy granola-y taste. It tastes best and works very well in things like pancakes, and such whole-grain items such as bran or corn muffins. It is perfect for oatmeal cookies, and the texture works for cookies in general, although the taste may be too pronounced for some. Chocolate cake-y recipes have mixed results, I would recommend only using one egg's worth of flax seed replacement in those, because the taste can be overpowering.

Tips:

Always store ground flax seeds in the freezer because they are highly perishable. This mixture is not only an excellent replacement for eggs, it also contributes vital omega-3 fatty acids.

Where to get flax seeds:

Health food stores

⋯❖ SILKEN TOFU

How to use it:

3 tablespoons blended silken tofu = 1 egg. Whizz in a blender until completely smooth and creamy, leaving no graininess or chunks. You will want to add other wet ingredients to this mixture to get it to blend properly. I recommend vacuum-packed extra-firm silken tofu.

When it works best:

Silken tofu works best in dense cakes and brownies, and in smaller quantities for lighter cakes and fluffy things (if the recipe calls for 3 eggs, use only 2 "tofu" eggs"). Whizzed tofu leaves virtually no taste, so it is an excellent replacer in delicate cake recipes where flax seeds would overpower the flavour. In cookie recipes, it may make the cookie more cake-y and fluffy than anticipated, so add 1 teaspoon of starch (such as arrowroot or cornflour) to the recipe to combat that. Silken tofu may make pancakes a little heavy, so it is not recommended for those, although it could work well with a little experimentation.

Where to get it:

Health food stores, and in some supermarkets.

⋯❖ ENER-G EGG REPLACER

How to use it:

1½ tablespoons Ener-G + 2 tablespoons water mixed well = 1 egg

Many people swear by this egg replacer. I think it is good to use in a pinch, in all baking that requires a few eggs. However, I can definitely taste it in cakes and cookies (tastes chalky), and I'm not crazy about the dense texture it turns out.

When it works best:

It seems to work best in cookies, or things that are supposed to be a little crispy.

Where to get it:

Health food stores, some supermarkets (look in baking or ethnic food section)

⤳ BANANA

How to use it:

½ banana blended until smooth or mashed well = 1 egg.

Bananas work wonders as an egg replacer in baking, which is the reason many banana bread recipes don't require eggs. They hold the air bubbles well, make things nice and moist, and impart a nice flavour. However, you don't want everything tasting like banana, so use in things where the taste won't be intrusive. I've also noticed that baked goods using banana brown very nicely, but sometimes you don't want your recipe to come out that brown.

When it works best:

Quick breads, muffins, cakes, pancakes

Tip:

Make sure bananas are nice and ripe and have started to brown.

Where to get it:

Just kidding, I think you can figure this one out.

⤳ SOY YOGURT

How to use it:

4 tablespoons soy yogurt = 1 egg.

Soy yogurt works a lot like whizzed tofu as an egg replacer. It makes things moist and yummy.

When it works best:

Quick breads, muffins, cakes

Where to get it:

Health food stores, yuppyish supermarkets

⋯⇴ LOSE THE MILK

This is a no-brainer. Use soy, rice, or almond milk. Buttermilk? Add a teaspoon of cider vinegar or lemon juice to your milk substitute and let it sit for a couple of minutes.

⋯⇴ IT'S LIKE BUTTAH...

Margarine

Instead of butter try unsalted dairy-free margarine or go ahead and use salted but reduce the amount of salt in the recipe. Lose 1/4 teaspoon of salt per 50g/2oz of margarine. But try to use the non-hydrogenated kind, I dunno, for your health?

Oil

My favourite thing to use instead of butter is rapeseed oil, but you can use any vegetable oil; just reduce the amount. If a recipe calls for 115g/4oz of butter, I use 5 tablepoons of oil.

MAKES 4 DOZEN COOKIES

These are soft out of the oven, but as they cool they are nice and chewy. I use ground flax seeds to make them a little chewier but it is an optional ingredient.

225g/8oz plain flour
125g/4oz rolled oats
1 teaspoon bicarbonate of soda
3/4 teaspoon salt
1 teaspoon cinnamon
1/2 teaspoon nutmeg
300g/11oz sugar
150ml/1/4 pint rapeseed oil
2 tablespoons molasses
250ml/8fl oz canned pumpkin, or cooked puréed pumpkin
1 teaspoon vanilla extract
1 tablespoon ground flax seeds (optional)
115g/4oz walnuts, finely chopped
65g/21/2oz raisins

> Preheat oven to 180°C/350°F/gas mark 4. Lightly grease two baking sheets.

> Mix together the flour, oats, bicarbonate of soda, salt, and spices.

> In a separate bowl, mix together the sugar, oil, molasses, pumpkin, and vanilla (and flax seeds if using) until very well combined. Add the dry ingredients to the wet in three batches, folding to combine. Fold in the walnuts and raisins.

> Drop by tablespoons onto the prepared baking sheets. They don't spread very much so they can be placed only 2.5cm/1in apart. Flatten the tops of the cookies with a fork or with your fingers, to press into a cookie shape. Bake for 16 minutes at 180°C/350°F/gas mark 4. If you are using two sheets of cookies on two levels of your oven, rotate the sheets halfway through for even baking. You'll have enough batter for four sheets.

> Remove from oven, cool on the baking sheets for 2 minutes, then transfer to a cooling rack. These taste best when they've had some time to cool and set. They taste even better the next day!

PUMPKIN OATMEAL COOKIES

BIG CRUNCHY PEANUT BUTTER-OATMEAL COOKIES

MAKES ABOUT 12 HUGE-ASS COOKIES

Terry baked these for a Post Punk Kitchen bake sale, and they went flying off the table, luckily no one was hurt. They're really peanut buttery and satisfying.

225g/8oz plain flour
175g/6oz rolled oats
2 teaspoons baking powder
1 teaspoon salt
175ml/6fl oz rapeseed oil
175g/6oz crunchy peanut butter (about 12 tablespoons)
200g/7oz granulated sugar
225g/8oz brown sugar
125ml/4fl oz vanilla soy milk
2 teaspoons vanilla extract

> Preheat oven to 180°C/350°F/gas mark 4. Lightly grease two baking sheets.

> Toss together the flour, oats, baking powder, and salt in a large mixing bowl. In a separate bowl mix together the oil, peanut butter, sugars, soy milk, and vanilla.

> Add the dry ingredients to the wet, and mix. The dough will be very firm and moist. For perfectly round, large cookies: pack 5 tablespoons dough into a cup, pop out and roll the dough into a firm ball and flatten just barely on a prepared baking sheet, spacing the dough balls well apart. Lightly grease the bottom of a glass or heavy ceramic plate; press the top of the cookies with the bottom of the pie plate to flatten to a 1cm/1/2in thickness. Leave about 2.5cm/1in between the flattened cookies as these will spread slightly. Bake for about 12 to 15 minutes till cookies have puffed a bit and are lightly browned. Allow to cool at least 10 minutes to firm up before moving off the baking sheet. You can also make normal-size cookies using 1 to 2 tablespoons of dough instead, baking these 8 to 10 minutes.

MAKES 2 DOZEN COOKIES

Cute, simple, crispy peanut butter cookies with a crosshatched top, perfect for munching on with a glass of soy milk.

5 tablespoons rapeseed oil
175g/6oz brown sugar
225g/8oz smooth, unsalted peanut butter
1 teaspoon vanilla extract
1 tablespoon cornflour
115g/4oz flour
1/2 teaspoon baking powder
1/8 teaspoon salt

> Preheat oven to 180°C/350°F/gas mark 4. Lightly grease two baking sheets.

> In a mixing bowl, cream together the oil, sugar, peanut butter, and vanilla. Add the cornflour and beat till well combined. Add the flour, baking powder, and salt; mix well.

> Drop the dough by rounded tablespoonfuls about 2.5cm/1in apart onto a prepared baking sheet and flatten each one a bit with the palm of your hand. Use the backside of a fork to press into each cookie, then press in the opposite direction to create a crosshatched pattern. Clean off the fork whenever it starts collecting too much dough. Bake for 12 minutes, let sit on the baking sheets to cool for about 3 minutes, transfer to cooling rack to cool.

CRISPY PEANUT BUTTER COOKIES

BUTTERY LEMON CUTOUT COOKIES

MAKES 2 DOZEN COOKIES

You can decorate these lemony delights with the simple White Icing (page 224), use a piping bag to make swirly or stripy shape, or simply sprinkle them with some sugar.

225g/8oz non-hydrogenated margarine, softened
75g/3oz icing sugar
175g/6oz plain flour
1 teaspoon vanilla extract
2 tablespoons finely grated lemon zest
1/4 teaspoon salt
Granulated sugar for sprinkling on the tops

> In a mixing bowl beat together the margarine and icing sugar until light and fluffy. Add the flour in 2 batches, beating well after each addition. Add the remaining ingredients and mix well. Mould the dough into a ball, wrap in clingfilm, and refrigerate for at least 2 hours, until firm.

> Preheat oven to 160°C/325°F/gas mark 3; line two baking sheets with parchment paper.

> Roll out dough on a lightly floured surface. Cut with 5cm/2in cookie cutters (heart and star shapes are awesome). Place the cookies 2.5cm/1in apart on the prepared baking sheets, sprinkle with granulated sugar, and bake for 6 to 8 minutes. Cool on the baking sheets for 2 minutes, then transfer to cooling racks to cool. Place the dough scraps in the fridge and roll them out again to make more cookies.

NO APOLOGY NECESSARY

I've had dinner parties where I spent practically the whole time explaining the meal to my guests, with all sorts of excuses as to what went wrong. "Well you see usually the dough is more tender but I let my cat mix the batter and you all know how cats can be..." One day I brought a batch of brownies to my office job and I was just done explaining to my colleagues why they weren't as fudgy as usual when my friend Jamie from Kentucky pulled me aside and said, "Never apologize for your food." I have taken that advice to heart and sure, if you use salt instead of sugar in your cookies then just don't serve them, but if things come out a little different from what you were expecting just go with it. Now that's Southern class.

FIG NOT-INS

MAKES 24 COOKIES

I love these cookie bar things. They are larger than your shop-bought fig sandwich cookies, but bigger is better, right? They're a great snack for a lunch box.

For the dough:

4 tablespoons non-hydrogenated margarine, softened
4 tablespoons non-hydrogenated shortening
150g/5oz sugar
2 tablespoons tapioca starch or arrowroot or cornflour
3 tablespoons rice or soy milk
2 teaspoons vanilla extract
225g/8oz plain flour
1/2 teaspoon baking powder
1/2 teaspoon bicarbonate of soda
1/2 teaspoon salt

For the filling:

450g/1lb dried figs, chopped
125ml/4fl oz water
4 tablespoons sugar
1 teaspoon finely grated lemon zest

Prepare the dough:

> In a mixing bowl, cream together the margarine, shortening, and sugar. Add the tapioca starch and mix well. Beat in the rice milk and vanilla. Add the flour, baking powder, bicarbonate of soda, and salt, and mix well. Divide the dough into two portions, wrap in clingfilm, and refrigerate for about an hour.

Prepare the filling:

> Combine all the filling ingredients in a saucepan. Bring to a boil, then lower the heat and simmer for 5 minutes or so, stirring often. Let cool before assembling the cookies for baking.

To prepare cookies:

> Preheat oven to 180°C/350°F/gas mark 4. Lightly grease a baking sheet.

> On a lightly floured surface, roll out one portion of the dough into a rectangle roughly 23 x 38cm/9 x 15in (you don't need to be too precise about it, it's OK if it's not perfectly rectangular). Divide the dough lengthwise into three equal strips. Place the three strips on a baking sheet 10cm/4in apart and divide the filling equally among the dough strips, creating a line of filling along the centre with 1cm/$\frac{1}{2}$in of space on either side of the filling.

> Roll out the second batch of dough to the same dimensions and cut into three strips. Place this dough over the filling-topped one and seal the edges by lightly pressing with your fingertips. Cut into 4cm/1$\frac{1}{2}$in lengths but don't separate them. Bake for about 18 minutes, until lightly browned. Let cool on baking sheet for 2 minutes, then cut each cookie again to separate and transfer to a cooling rack to cool completely.

CHOCOLATE THUMBPRINT COOKIES

MAKES 2 DOZEN COOKIES

People love thumbprint cookies. The name and the little dollop of jam always elicit awwws from the masses.

115g/4oz plain flour
5 tablespoons cocoa powder
1/4 teaspoon salt
1/4 teaspoon bicarbonate of soda
5 tablespoons groundnut oil
5 tablespoons soy milk
1 teaspoon vanilla extract
1/2 teaspoon almond extract
130g/4 1/2oz sugar
6 teaspoons jam (I like raspberry or apricot)

> Preheat oven to 180°C/350°F/gas mark 4; line two baking sheets with parchment paper.

> Sift together the flour, cocoa powder, salt, and bicarbonate of soda.

> In a large bowl mix together all the wet ingredients (except the jam) plus the sugar. Add the dry ingredients to the wet and incorporate well.

> With damp hands, roll 1 tablespoon of dough into a ball and press between your palms into a disc, then place on a prepared baking sheet. It's important to the texture of the cookies that your hands are damp, to prevent cracking at the edges. Bake the cookies for 5 minutes, then remove from oven. Press your thumb into each cookie to make an indent. They're pretty hot at this point so proceed carefully, or use something thumblike to make the indent. Place 1/4 teaspoon of jam into each indentation. Bake another 6 minutes. Remove from oven and let sit for two minutes, then transfer to a cooling rack to cool.

MAKES 16 BARS

These are blondies topped with a raspberry spread and chocolate chips, then finished off with some of the blondie batter dropped on top. They're tantalizing and cool looking and kids seem to really enjoy them. If you are low on time you can use 275g/10oz raspberry jam in place of the raspberry layer.

For raspberry layer:
350g/12oz frozen raspberries
3 tablespoons tapioca starch (you can substitute arrowroot
   or cornflour)
3 tablespoons cold water
5 tablespoons sugar

For the blondie layer:
425g/15oz plain flour
1¼ teaspoons bicarbonate of soda
½ teaspoon salt
175g/6oz plain or vanilla soy yogurt
3 tablespoons rice milk
125ml/4fl oz plus 2 tablespoons rapeseed oil
400g/14oz sugar
1 tablespoon vanilla extract
150g/5oz chocolate chips

> Preheat oven to 180°C/350°F/gas mark 4. Lightly grease a 23 x 33cm/9 x 13in baking tin.

Prepare the raspberry layer:

> In a saucepan combine all raspberry layer ingredients and stir until the tapioca starch is dissolved. Bring to a boil and then lower to a low boil, stirring often, for 5 minutes or until thickened. Remove from heat.

Prepare the blondie layer:

> In a mixing bowl sift together the flour, bicarbonate of soda, and salt. In a separate bowl, combine the soy yogurt, rice milk, oil, sugar, and vanilla. In batches, mix the dry ingredients into the wet to form a dough. Set aside 250ml/8fl oz of the dough and spread the rest in the prepared baking tin. Spread the raspberry layer over it (or use raspberry jam). Sprinkle half of the chocolate chips over the raspberry layer. Drop the remaining dough over the chips and raspberries; sprinkle the rest of the chocolate chips over that. Bake for 35 minutes. Let cool completely before serving.

MAKES 12 BROWNIES

This is a really fudgy brownie with a banana pudding on top that melts into the brownie layer and forms this unbelievable ooey gooey banana brownie concoction. Although you can hold it in your hand, you may want to serve it with a fork.

For the brownies:
115g/4oz plain chocolate, chopped
2 large very ripe bananas, mashed
5 tablespoons rapeseed oil
250ml/8fl oz sugar
1 teaspoon vanilla extract
90g/3¹/₂oz plain flour
25g/1oz cocoa powder
1/4 teaspoon bicarbonate of soda
1/8 teaspoon salt

For the topping layer:
2 large very ripe bananas, mashed
2 tablespoons sugar
3 tablespoons soy milk
1/2 teaspoon vanilla extract
1 tablespoon arrowroot powder

For decoration and more banana yumminess:
1 ripe but not very ripe banana, thinly sliced

To make the brownie batter:

> Melt the chocolate by placing in a pan or heat-proof mixing bowl over a small pan of boiling water. Stir with a heatproof spatula until completely melted, then remove from heat and set aside to cool.

> In a large mixing bowl, combine the mashed bananas, the oil, and the sugar. Use a handheld mixer to beat everything together for about a minute. If you don't have a mixer, use a strong fork and mix for about 3 minutes. Mix in the vanilla and the melted chocolate.

> In a separate bowl, sift together the flour, cocoa powder, bicarbonate of soda, and salt. Add this to the banana mixture in batches, mixing with the hand mixer as you go along. Mix for about 1 minute more.

Prepare the banana topping:

> In a small bowl, combine all topping ingredients and mix with the hand mixer (remember to rinse the beaters off first) for about a minute.

To assemble and bake the brownies:

> Spread the brownie batter evenly into a baking tin. Pour the banana topping over that and spread evenly. Bake for 30 minutes. Remove from oven and let cool. After about 15 minutes, move it to the fridge until fully cooled. Cut into twelve squares, place a few slices of banana on top of each portion, and serve.

MAKES 16 BLONDIES

Macadamias make these blondies rich and buttery. They are great un-iced if you don't want something too sweet but the caramel-maple topping makes for a decadent treat.

For the blondies:
300g/11oz plain flour
1 teaspoon baking powder
1 teaspoon bicarbonate of soda
1/2 teaspoon salt
175g/6oz firm silken tofu
3 tablespoons rice or soy milk
5 tablespoons rapeseed oil
400g/14oz sugar
2 tablespoons vanilla extract
150g/5oz raw macadamias, partially chopped and partially ground
    (see Punk Points on page 208)

For the topping:
4 tablespoons non-hydrogenated margarine
2 tablespoons demerara or other brown sugar
3 tablepoons pure maple syrup
115g/4oz raw macadamia nuts, coarsely chopped

> Preheat oven to 180°C/350°F/gas mark 4. Lightly grease a 23 x 33cm/9 x 13in baking tin.

To prepare the dough:

> In a large bowl, sift together the flour, baking powder, bicarbonate of soda, and salt.

> In a blender, whizz the tofu with the rice milk until smooth. Add the oil, sugar, and vanilla, and blend again. Pour the tofu mixture into the flour mixture and use a firm wooden spoon to combine everything well. Fold in the macadamias. The batter will be thick and have a cookie dough consistency. Spread in the baking tin and bake for 25 minutes. Meanwhile, prepare the topping.

To prepare the topping:

> In a saucepan over medium heat, combine the margarine, demerara sugar, and maple syrup, and heat until the sugar dissolves. Increase the heat to bring to a boil for 1 minute. Stir in the nuts. Remove from heat.

> Remove the blondies from oven and pour the topping over them, return to oven, and bake for 10 more minutes.

> Let cool completely before serving, the topping should harden to a caramel-like consistency. I cut these into sixteen squares but they are also fine as triangles.

┈┤ PUNK POINTS

> The macadamias should be partially ground and partially chopped, which is easily achieved in a food processor with about 30 pulses. If you don't have a food processor then chop all the macadamias, put half of them aside, and continue to chop the others or grind them in a blender until they resemble coarse crumbs.

DATE-NUT DIAMONDS

MAKES ABOUT 20 BARS

OK, you don't have to cut these into diamonds, but they look good if you choose to. These bars are very *Home and Garden*.

115g/4oz plus 2 tablespoons plain flour
1/8 teaspoon salt
115g/4oz non-hydrogenated margarine
130g/4 1/2oz dried dates, roughly chopped
175g/6oz brown sugar
115g/4oz chopped walnuts
40g/1 1/2oz desiccated coconut
1 teaspoon vanilla extract
2 tablespoons tapioca starch

> Preheat oven to 190°C/375°F/gas mark 5. Lightly grease an 28 x 42cm/11 x 17in baking tin.

> In a medium-size bowl combine 115g/4oz flour and the salt. Cut in the margarine using a pastry knife or your fingers until you've got coarse crumbs. Press the mixture into the bottom of the prepared pan. Bake for 12 minutes.

> In a small saucepan place the dates in enough water to cover. Bring to a boil; reduce heat, cover, and simmer for 10 minutes; drain.

> In a mixing bowl stir together the cooked dates, brown sugar, walnuts, coconut, and vanilla. Sprinkle with the tapioca starch and stir till combined. Spread evenly over the partially baked crust. Bake for 15 minutes. Remove from oven and let cool. Cut into diamonds by slicing strips lengthwise, then diagonally.

DESSERTS

FINALLY, DESSERT! THE MOST COMMON COOKING COMPLAINT I HEAR FROM PEOPLE IS THAT THEY CAN'T BAKE. I DON'T KNOW WHAT THE PROBLEM IS BUT WOULDN'T IT BE WORTH IT TO LEARN SO THAT YOU CAN HAVE CAKES AND PUDDINGS AND PIES? GET AN OVEN THERMOMETER, A TIMER, AND APPROPRIATE TINS AND I ASSURE YOU, YOU CAN BAKE! THIS CHAPTER IS DEFINITELY MY BABY AND THE ONE I FOUND MYSELF TESTING THE RECIPES FOR OVER AND OVER AND OVER AGAIN. ENJOY!

BAKE SALES

The election of 2004 was hard on everyone. The day John Kerry lost I went to Prospect Park and sat in the middle of the field. I took comfort in the feeling of the grass and dirt below me as I sat alone in the empty meadow and I was a bit scared to leave because
I thought that in my liberal neighbourhood there would be panic on the streets.

Months later people were still analyzing why he lost. Was it fear? Was it homophobia? Was it bible-thumping? I thought back to what the lefties did "wrong" and the only thing that I could really put my finger on was this one "Baking against Bush" bake sale I went to. There were actually shop-bought items, wrapped in plastic. Good people, that is not a bake sale. I am sure that in Texas, if they were to hold a "Baking for Bush" bake sale, there would be no factory-baked cakes. In fact, I am sure something like that would rank right up there with gay marriage. If we as a movement want to succeed, our bake sales must reflect that. We must have fresh-baked cookies, cakes loaded with icing. We must take the time to pipe those gingerbread decorations with all our might. Otherwise we are in the business of reselling capitalism. Our bake sales must come from our hearts and our ovens (at the correct temperatures) in order for us to be taken seriously. In this chapter I've included some items that will help usher in the revolution.

SERVES 12

If I were to make a commercial for this carrot cake it would feature a calypso band in the dining room and kids dancing, heck even grandma joins in the dance. What I am saying is that this is not your average carrot cake. Feel free to replace the macadamia nuts with their more affordable cousins, walnuts.

260g/9^1/$_2$ oz plain flour
1 tablespoon baking powder
1 teaspoon bicarbonate of soda
^{3}/$_4$ teaspoon salt
2 teaspoons ground cinnamon
^{1}/$_2$ teaspoon ground or freshly grated nutmeg
250ml/8fl oz pineapple juice
125ml/4fl oz rapeseed oil
155g/5oz sugar
120ml/4fl oz pure maple syrup
2 teaspoons vanilla extract
115g/4oz macadamia nuts, roughly chopped
4 tablespoons crystallized ginger, chopped
   (even better if you can find small pieces specifically for baking)
75g/3oz desiccated coconut
250g/8oz carrots, grated

> Preheat oven to 180°C/350°F/gas mark 4. Have ready two 20cm/8in round springform cake tins, lightly greased. Alternatively, this could be made in a 23 x 33cm/9 x 13in baking tin and cut in half lengthwise to create two layers or just iced as one layer.

> In a large mixing bowl sift together the flour, baking powder, bicarbonate of soda, salt, and ground spices.

> In a separate large mixing bowl, mix together the pineapple, oil, sugar, maple syrup, and vanilla. Add the dry ingredients to the wet in batches, and combine well with a hand mixer or strong fork. Fold in the macadamias, ginger, coconut, and carrots.

> Divide the batter evenly between the two round cake tins, or spread in the rectangular tin, and bake for 40 to 45 minutes. Let cool in pans. Remove from pans and put a layer of coconut icing (page 221) between the layers, and another layer of coconut icing on top; I like to leave the sides free of icing because it looks pretty.

GINGER-MACADAMIA-COCONUT-CARROT CAKE

RASPBERRY BLACKOUT CAKE WITH GANACHE-Y ICING

SERVES 12

This makes a great birthday cake and I have found that even people who think that they aren't crazy about chocolate and raspberries go crazy over it. The recipe calls for a lot of icing (recipe follows) because I'm hoping that you will get a piping bag and have some fun decorating the top with chocolate roses. If I am wrong and you absolutely will not, then you can get away with halving the icing recipe.

175g/6oz plain flour
50g/2oz cocoa powder
1 teaspoon baking powder
1 teaspoon bicarbonate of soda
1/2 teaspoon salt
350ml/12fl oz plain rice or soy milk
125ml/4fl oz rapeseed oil
275g/10oz raspberry preserves (reserve half for the batter)
2 teaspoons vanilla extract
250g/9oz sugar
Fresh raspberries for decorating and yumminess

> Preheat oven to 180°C/350°F/gas mark 4. Spray two 20cm/8in round springform cake tins with cooking spray. If you don't have springform then use parchment paper rounds on the bottom of two ordinary 20cm/8in round cake tins to prevent sticking.

> Sift together the flour, cocoa powder, baking powder, bicarbonate of soda, and salt. Combine the rice milk, oil, half the jam, the vanilla, and the sugar in a large bowl and mix with a hand mixer or strong fork. The jam should be mostly dissolved with the rest of the ingredients; some small clumps are OK. Add the dry ingredients to the wet in batches and mix until everything is incorporated. Divide the batter between the prepared tins and bake at 180°C/ 350°F/gas mark 4 for 40 to 45 minutes, or until a cocktail stick or knife comes out clean. Remove from oven and let cool in tins.

> When the cakes have cooled fully, spread one layer of cake with a thin layer of the reserved raspberry jam (give the jam a quick mix with a strong fork to get a spreadable consistency); spread a layer of chocolate icing on top of the jam. Place the other layer of cake on top and spread its top with jam. Carefully spread the chocolate icing over the top, then ice the sides. I like to put a circle of fresh raspberries around the circumference of the top. If you happen to have a piping bag and nozzles around, you can alternate a rosebud or star flourish with a raspberry, and a few raspberries in the centre will finish it off.

CHOCOLATE GANACHE-Y ICING

175ml/6fl oz soy cream
6 tablespoons non-hydrogenated margarine
275g/10oz plain chocolate chips

> In a saucepan over medium heat, bring the soy cream to a low boil. Add the margarine and melt, turn off the heat, and stir in chocolate chips until smooth. Let sit for at least 1 hour. It should still have a pourable consistency at this point. If you want a spreadable consistency then refrigerate for an hour. (If you refrigerate it for more than a few hours, it sets too much to spread easily, so you will need to reheat it, then let it sit at room temperature before using.)

ORANGE-RUM TEA CAKE

SERVES 8

This is a nice intensely orange cake perfect as an afternoon cake whilst you take tea with your like-minded friends. There's no icing, just a simple orange rum syrup that takes all of three minutes to put together, and it forms a nice caramelly base for the slivered almonds. If you don't have a 23cm/9in springform tin, a smaller round tin works well; just increase the baking time by about 10 minutes and use parchment paper to prevent sticking. You will need about six oranges to get the amount of juice needed.

For the cake:
175g/6oz soy yogurt
5 tablespoons oil
150g/5oz sugar
3 tablespoons soy milk
3 tablespoons freshly squeezed orange juice
4 teaspoons finely grated fresh orange zest
1 teaspoon vanilla extract
150g/5oz plain flour
4 tablepoons yellow cornmeal
1 1/2 teaspoons baking powder
1/2 teaspoon salt
50g/2oz slivered almonds

For orange rum syrup:
5 tablespoons freshly squeezed orange juice
2 tablespoons sugar
2 tablespoons rum

> Preheat oven to 180°C/350°F/gas mark 4. Spray your cake tin with nonstick cooking spray or lightly grease with oil.

> In a large bowl, mix together the soy yogurt, oil, and sugar. Add the soy milk, orange juice, orange zest, and vanilla. Mix well to combine.

> I like to sift the dry ingredients directly into the wet at this point, but you can also use a separate bowl to sift together the flour, cornmeal, baking powder, and salt, and then add that to the wet mixture, and mix to combine.

> Transfer the batter to the prepared baking tin and bake until golden, when a cocktail stick or knife inserted in the centre comes out clean, about 35 minutes.

> Remove from oven and let cool 10 minutes or until you can handle the pan and remove the cake; let it cool upside down or on a cooling rack. At this point you should prepare the syrup.

> In a small saucepan, bring the orange juice and sugar to a boil over medium-high heat, stirring constantly until the sugar is dissolved. Lower the heat to a simmer, add the rum, and simmer for 2 more minutes. Remove from heat and let cool completely.

> When the cake has cooled completely, place on a serving plate and arrange the slivered almonds on top. Pour the cooled orange syrup over the top; let sit for a couple of minutes to absorb the syrup. Serve.

CHOCOLATE-RUM PUDDING CAKE

SERVES 8–10

I found a recipe like this in a cookbook for one-bowl desserts and decided to veganize it. The rum flavour isn't overpowering at all, it just adds a little hint of sumthin' sumthin'. You can serve it warm with the pudding layer oozing all over the place, or serve it chilled with the pudding layer nice and thick on the top. It's a quick recipe that will make people think it took more work than it really did. If you are a pathological liar, just go ahead and let them think that.

115g/4oz plain flour
2 teaspoons baking powder
1/2 teaspoon bicarbonate of soda
1/4 teaspoon salt
200g/7oz sugar
50g/2oz cocoa powder
125ml/4fl oz plain soy milk
3 tablespoons rapeseed oil
1 teaspoon vanilla extract
1 teaspoon rum extract
   (or just use 1 more teaspoon vanilla if you don't have rum extract)
125ml/4fl oz pure maple syrup
3 tablespoons light rum
125ml/4fl oz boiling water

> Boil some water in a kettle, preheat oven to 180°C/350°F/gas mark 4, and grease a 23cm/9in round springform cake tin.

> Sift together the flour, baking powder, bicarbonate of soda, salt, 150g/5oz of the sugar, and half the cocoa powder. Add the soy milk, oil, and extracts, and mix into a thick batter. Spread the batter in the prepared cake tin. Sprinkle the top with the remaining cocoa powder and sugar. Pour 125ml/4fl oz of boiling water into a glass measuring jug, add the maple syrup and rum to the water, and pour this mixture on top of the cake batter.

> Place the cake on a baking sheet in case of pudding overflow and bake for 30 to 35 minutes. Let cool just a bit; while it's still warm, place the cake on a large plate and release the sides (your plate should have a slight rim to prevent spillage). Throw on a scoop of vanilla soy ice cream if you like and you've got yourself one impressive dessert.

LET YOU EAT CAKE

I'm a chubby girl. I say it proudly and with no bad feelings. I'm happy with my body (except for those days when I hate it) but sometimes my weight pushes past my comfort zone (writing cookbooks doesn't help this) and I need to lose a few pounds. Losing weight doesn't mean I have to stop eating cookies and cakes, it just means I have to change how I prepare them and then somehow get myself to consume only one. So if you, too, occasionally bust out of your bullet belt, here are some tips for healthier baking.

Making your baked foods low fat is really super-duper easy. I'm almost ashamed to write about it because it's such a gimme. There are two fat substitutes that I use: puréed prunes or apple sauce. The great thing about these fat replacers is that they also work as binding agents (meaning they help hold the cake together), so it's a win-win situation. Generally, I use the prunes in chocolate things and the apple sauce in anything that isn't chocolate. The apple sauce doesn't usually leave any sort of a taste but the prunes give a somewhat "healthy" (for lack of a better word) taste to things, but it adds a nice dimension to chocolate things. Don't be afraid to convert any of the baked goods in this book; I have made them all low fat at one point or another and I know that it will work.

For prunes, if the recipe calls for 125ml/4fl oz oil or 115g/4oz margarine, then weigh out 75g/3oz prunes and place in a bowl. I wouldn't advise using any more than that because it may make the finished product too moist. Hold the prunes down with your hand so that they don't float up, and add the apple juice or water or whatever liquid you might be using in the recipe (soy or rice milk, for instance). Then transfer to a blender and purée until very smooth. For apple sauce, follow the same guideline. Use 5 tablespoons of apple sauce in place of 125ml/4fl oz oil or 115g/4oz margarine. Expect the finished product to be cakier than usual. Whether I choose prunes or apple sauce I always add 2 teaspoons of oil to the recipe at the point when the liquids are combined with the dry ingredients. It's a small amount but goes a long way to improving the texture. I also remove 2 tablespoons of sugar for every 120ml/4fl oz of prune purée used.

Fibre is also an important factor in weight loss. White flour has very little fibre, and you lose a lot of the nutrients from the original grain. I like to use wholemeal flour instead; it will work wonderfully in all your sweet baked treats. Use it in place of plain flour. I often use half wholemeal flour and half plain flour.

So go ahead and have that cookie, and if you are scared you will eat all of them in the middle of the night just send them my way.

BLUEBERRY COFFEE CAKE

MAKES 16 SQUARES

In my country, coffee cake doesn't actually have any coffee in it, it's just a cake that goes well with coffee. I had to quit coffee anyway, so I eat my cake with tea, although in my heart of hearts I know it's a coffee cake. This is the perfect treat if you want to get warm fuzzies inside.

For the topping:
4 tablespoons plain flour
3 tablespoons brown sugar
1/4 teaspoon ground cinnamon
1 tablespoon rapeseed oil
115g/4oz chopped walnuts

For the cake:
450g/1lb plain flour
1 tablespoon baking powder
1 teaspoon bicarbonate of soda
1 1/2 teaspoons salt
1 1/2 teaspoons ground cinnamon
4 teaspoon ground allspice
3 tablespoons rapeseed oil
175g/6oz vanilla soy yogurt
250ml/8fl oz pure maple syrup
350ml/12fl oz plain soy milk
1 teaspoon vanilla extract
225g/8oz fresh blueberries

> Preheat oven to 180°C/350°F/gas mark 4. Lightly grease or spray a 23 x 33cm/9 x 13in baking tin with nonstick cooking spray.

Make the topping:

> Sift together the flour, brown sugar, and cinnamon. Drizzle in the oil a little at a time and mix with your fingertips until crumbs form. Add the walnuts and mix.

Make the cake:

> Sift together the dry ingredients into a large bowl. In a separate bowl, vigorously whisk together the wet ingredients until well combined. Add the wet ingredients to the dry and mix well. Fold in the blueberries.

> Spread the batter in the prepared tin and sprinkle the topping over it. Bake for 45 minutes, or until a cocktail stick or knife comes out clean. Tastes great still warm.

··> PUNK POINTS

> You can substitute frozen blueberries for fresh but keep them in the freezer till the last possible moment to prevent thawing that might turn the batter purple.

INTERVIEW WITH A CUPCAKE LOVER

This is an interview I did for the cupcakelicious blog—Cupcakes Take the Cake (www.cupcakestakethecake.blogspot.com/)

Name: Isa Chandra Moskowitz
Age: 32
Location: Prospect Heights, Brooklyn
Occupation: Wage slave and Celebrity Chef of the People
Web site: www.theppk.com

How often do you eat cupcakes? At least once a week.

What's the best thing about eating cupcakes? They say that the first thing you eat with is your eyes, and I really like to look at my cupcake first. I think most other people do, too. When you hand someone a slice of cake, sure, they're happy, but hand them a cupcake and they are dazzled. They spin it around and look at it from every angle.

What's your favourite type of cupcake? I've been on a citrus kick lately, but it's just a phase. I like a cupcake with ganache icing.

Favourite place to get cupcakes? Well veganism makes cupcake procurement a mite difficult. Veg City Diner used to have them but they've gone out of business. I usually make them myself so my answer would have to be "in my kitchen."

How do cupcakes compare/contrast to other baked goods for you? If there's a cupcake option I would choose that above all others. Cupcake eating is more of an experience or an activity. With other baked goods you're just having dessert.

Any other thoughts on the topic? My childhood cat was named Cupcake, she went to kitty heaven in 2000. I think of her every time I eat a cupcake.

MAKES 12 CUPCAKES

These are a must for the coconut lovers in your life: dense coconut cupcakes topped off with fluffy coconut icing to die for.

For the cupcakes:
115g/4oz plain flour
1/2 teaspoon baking powder
1/2 teaspoon bicarbonate of soda
1/4 teaspoon salt
50ml/2fl oz rapeseed oil
250ml/8fl oz coconut milk
150g/5oz sugar
1 teaspoon vanilla extract
75g/3oz desiccated coconut

For the icing:
4 tablespoons non-hydrogenated margarine at room temperature
3 tablespoons coconut milk
1 teaspoon vanilla extract
225g/8oz icing sugar, sifted
75g/3oz desiccated coconut

Bake the cupcakes:

> Preheat oven to 180°C/350°F/gas mark 4. Line a twelve-hole muffin tin with paper cake cases, set aside.

> Sift together the flour, baking powder, bicarbonate of soda, and salt. In a separate bowl combine the oil, coconut milk, sugar, and vanilla. Pour the dry ingredients into the wet and mix until smooth. Fold in the coconut. Use an ice-cream scoop to fill each paper case about two-thirds full. Bake at 180°C/350°F/gas mark 4 for 20 to 22 minutes; the cupcakes should be slightly browned around the edges and spring back when touched. Remove from the tin and place on a cooling rack.

Make the icing:

> Cream the margarine until light and fluffy. Add the coconut milk and vanilla and combine. Add the sifted icing sugar and mix until smooth (use an electric handheld mixer; otherwise it might take a good 5 minutes to mix). Add the coconut and combine. Refrigerate until ready to use.

> Ice when the cupcakes have cooled fully. You can sprinkle a little more coconut on top if you like, or put a berry on for some colour.

LEMON GEM CUPCAKES

MAKES 1 DOZEN CUPCAKES

These are sophisticated cupcakes. They don't peek over the wrapper; the icing comes right to the top. Once baked the cupcake gives off an iridescent glow, but don't worry, you are not living in a postapocalyptic world of glowing food, it's just the abundance of the lemon.

165g/5^1/$_2$oz plain flour
^{1}/$_2$ teaspoon baking powder
^{3}/$_4$ teaspoon bicarbonate of soda
^{1}/$_4$ teaspoon salt
3 tablespoons rapeseed oil
170g/6oz sugar
250ml/8fl oz rice milk
1 teaspoon vanilla extract
3 tablespoons lemon juice
1 tablespoon lemon zest

> Preheat oven to 180°C/350°F/gas mark 4. Line a twelve-hole muffin tin with paper cake cases.

> Sift together the flour, baking powder, bicarbonate of soda, and salt. In a separate bowl combine the oil, sugar, rice milk, vanilla, lemon juice, and lemon zest. Pour the dry ingredients into the wet and mix until smooth. Fill each cake case about two-thirds full; bake for 17 to 20 minutes. Remove the cupcakes from the muffin tin and place on a cooling rack. Ice when cooled fully.

LEMON ICING

3 tablespoons non-hydrogenated soy margarine, softened
3 tablespoons soy milk
2 tablespoons lemon juice
225g/8oz icing sugar, sifted

> Whisk the margarine with a fork until fluffy. Stir in the soy milk and lemon juice; add the icing sugar and mix until smooth. (It may take 5 minutes or so to get it to be the right consistency unless you use an electric handheld mixer). Refrigerate until ready to use.

MAKES 12 CUPCAKES

If I could only eat one cupcake for the rest of my life, well, first I would wonder what I did to deserve such punishment, and then I would choose these. And I think I know someone that would agree with me— the entire country of America. They take a long time, there are many steps, but they are so worth it. Don't skip the sifting step; the cocoa tends to clump up, and no one likes clumps. The recipe doubles really well, so go ahead and make a double batch.

115g/4oz plain flour
7 tablespoons cocoa powder
1 teaspoon baking powder
1/2 teaspoon bicarbonate of soda
1/4 teaspoon salt
250ml/8fl oz plain rice or soy milk
3 tablespoons rapeseed oil
125ml/4fl oz pure maple syrup
4 tablespoons sugar
1 teaspoon cider vinegar
1 teaspoon vanilla extract

> Preheat oven to 180°C/350°F/gas mark 4. Line a twelve-hole muffin tin with paper cake cases, spray the cases with rapeseed cooking spray.

> In a medium-size mixing bowl, sift together the flour, cocoa powder, baking powder, bicarbonate of soda, and salt. In a large mixing bowl combine the rice milk, oil, maple syrup, sugar, vinegar, and vanilla, and beat at medium speed with an electric handheld mixer for a good 2 minutes. Add the dry ingredients to the wet in two batches, mixing as you go. Beat for about a minute more.

> Use a wet ice-cream scoop to fill the paper cake cases three-quarters full. Bake for about 28 minutes, until a cocktail stick inserted in the centre comes out clean. Transfer to a cooling rack. Time to make the Fluffy White Icing.

FLUFFY WHITE ICING

4 tablespoons non-hydrogenated margarine
115g/4oz non-hydrogenated shortening
170g/6oz caster sugar
4 tablespoons plain soy milk powder
   (don't use low-fat, it has a "taste")
2 teaspoons vanilla extract (get the highest quality you can;
   the kind that's thick and syrupy tastes best)
Pinch salt

> In a medium-size mixing bowl, beat together the margarine and shortening with an electric handheld mixer on medium speed until well combined. Add the sugar and soy milk powder and beat for a good 10 minutes until very fluffy. Add vanilla extract and a pinch of salt, and beat for another minute. You may want to do a little taste test and add a little more sugar if needed. On to the Ganache:

CHOCOLATE GANACHE ICING

5 tablespoons soy milk
115g/4oz plain chocolate, chopped
2 tablespoons pure maple syrup

> In a small saucepan, scorch the soy milk (bring it to a boil), then lower the heat to a simmer and add the chocolate and maple syrup. Mix with a heatproof spatula for about 30 seconds. Turn the heat off, and continue stirring until the chocolate is fully melted and the icing is smooth. Next, make the icing for the squigglies:

ROYAL ICING FOR THE SQUIGGLIES

225g/8oz icing sugar
2 tablespoons soy milk powder
2 tablespoons water

> Sift the sugar into a mixing bowl. Add the soy milk powder.
Add 1 tablespoon of the water and stir, then add the rest of the water
a little bit at a time until you reach a consistency slightly more solid
than toothpaste. The icing should not be drippy at all; if it is add a
little more icing sugar.

Assemble the cupcakes:

> You will need two piping bags, one fitted with a small round nozzle
(the kind you use for writing) and one fitted with a large star-shaped
or round nozzle.

> Fill the large nozzle with Fluffy White Icing; fill the writing one
with Royal Icing.

> Poke a hole in the centre of each cupcake, using your little finger.
Fill the bag with the Fluffy White Icing and squeeze to get as much
icing into each hole as you can, slowly drawing out the bag, until the
icing fills to the top of the hole.

> Wipe the excess icing off the top of the cupcake with a napkin or
(if you're me) your finger.

> Dip the top of each cupcake into the Chocolate Ganache Icing.
Tilt the pan to add more depth to the icing for easier cupcake coating.
Place all the cupcakes on a chopping board, make some room in
your fridge, and put the cupcakes in there to set the ganache, about
10 minutes.

> Use these 10 minutes to practice your squigglies for the tops. I use
my left hand to steady my writing hand by holding onto my right
wrist. Practice a bit and see what works for you.

> Remove the cupcakes from the fridge and make your squigglies on
the top of the ganache. Return to the fridge to set. I like to keep the
cupcakes in there till I'm ready to serve them.

NO-BAKE BLACK BOTTOM-PEANUT BUTTER SILK PIE

SERVES 8

Peanut butter and chocolate. Need I say more? OK, this is rich, creamy, and what's more you don't have to bake it. I listed the milks to use in order of preference; I have made it with all four and I like coconut milk the best, but it's good with the others as well.

1 prepared Chocolate Cookie Pie Crust (recipe follows)
   or digestive biscuit crust

For chocolate coating:
115g/4oz plain chocolate
3 tablespoons rice or soy milk

For the filling:
350g/12oz extra-firm silken tofu
175g/6oz smooth peanut butter
175g/6oz icing sugar
2 teaspoons vanilla extract
150ml/1/4 pint coconut milk, soy cream, rice milk, or soy milk
300ml/1/2 pint boiling water
3 tablespoons agar

Prepare the chocolate coating:

> Melt the chocolate in a makeshift double boiler (page 204). When the chocolate has melted, add the soy milk and whisk until smooth. Remove from heat. Pour most of this mixture into the prepared pie crust, reserving a couple of tablespoons to drizzle over the top of the pie. Transfer the chocolate-coated pie crust to the fridge.

Make the filling:

> Combine the tofu, peanut butter, sugar, and vanilla in a blender or food processor. Blend until smooth.

> In a saucepan over moderate heat, boil the agar in 300ml/1/2 pint boiling water. Stir constantly until dissolved. This takes about 10 minutes. When dissolved, pour into a glass measuring jug (if you have only plastic, let the mixture cool just a bit before pouring it into the jug, so it doesn't melt the plastic).

> There is usually 75ml/21/2fl oz agar at this point. You want the liquids to be 250ml/8floz but you can't add it to the agar mixture or it will firm up, so if you have 75ml/21/2fl oz agar and water, add 150ml/1/4 pint of milk to the tofu mixture and blend. Then add the agar and blend again.

Assemble the pie:

Slowly pour the peanut butter mixture into the pie crust. Drizzle the remaining chocolate over the pie. Run a butter knife through the chocolate in straight lines to create a pretty pattern. Refrigerate, wrapped in clingfilm, for at least 3 hours.

NO-BAKE CHOCOLATE COOKIE PIE CRUST

You can use any chocolate wafer biscuits to make this simple crust. I like to use Nature's Path Deep Chocolate Cookies.

130g/4^1/$_2$oz chocolate wafers, crushed
2 tablespoons sugar
^{1}/$_8$ teaspoon salt
3 tablespoons rapeseed oil
1 tablespoon rice or soy milk

> In a food processor fitted with a steel blade, or a blender, combine the wafers, sugar, and salt. Pulse into fine crumbs. Remove from the processor and pour into a pie plate. Drizzle with the rapeseed oil and mix with your fingers. Drizzle with the soy milk and mix with your fingers. Press into the pie plate. Refrigerate until ready to use.

SWEET POTATO PIE WITH THREE-NUT TOPPING

SERVES 8–12

This is one of the first recipes I ever got off the Internet and veganized, so it is close to my heart. I love the combination of the three nuts but you can improvise with just one nut of your choosing; pecans are a great choice. Some people think sweet potatoes should only be a side dish and not a dessert; those people are not to be trusted so keep your distance.

For the digestive biscuit crust:
40g/1½oz walnuts, toasted
40g/1½oz hazelnuts, toasted
40g/1½oz almonds, toasted
225g/8oz digestive biscuits
4 tablespoons dark brown sugar
Pinch each of ground ginger, nutmeg, cinnamon, and allspice
5 tablespoons rapeseed oil

For the filling:
500g/1¼lb sweet potatoes
2 tablespoons arrowroot
90g/3½oz sugar
125ml/4fl oz soy milk
3 tablespoons rapeseed oil
2 tablespoons pure maple syrup
175g/6oz firm silken tofu
1 teaspoon ground ginger
½ teaspoon ground nutmeg
½ teaspoon ground cinnamon
¼ teaspoon ground allspice
⅛ teaspoon ground cloves

For the topping:
4 tablespoons non-hydrogenated margarine
4 tablespoons brown sugar
2 tablespoons maple syrup
40g/1½oz whole almonds, toasted
40g/1½oz whole hazelnuts, toasted
40g/1½oz walnuts, toasted

> Preheat oven to 180°C/350°F/gas mark 4. Bake the sweet potatoes until tender, about 1 hour. Meanwhile, make the crust.

Make the crust:

> Grind the nuts in a food processor, crumble in the digestive biscuits, and grind into crumbs. Add the sugar and spices, pulse to combine. Add the oil and pulse to moisten the crumbs. Press into a 23cm/9in (preferably glass) pie plate, set aside.

Make the filling:

> When the sweet potatoes are done, remove them from the oven and let them cool. Purée in a food processor or blender. Add all other filling ingredients and purée until smooth. Pour the filling into the crust. Bake at 180°C/350°F/gas mark 4 until the centre moves only slightly when the dish is shaken, covering with foil if the crust browns too quickly, about 40 minutes.

> While the pie bakes, prepare the topping:

Make the topping:

> Stir the margarine, sugar, and maple syrup in heavy medium-size saucepan over low heat until the sugar dissolves. Increase the heat and boil for 1 minute. Mix in the nuts, coating them completely.

> Spoon the hot nut mixture over the pie. Continue baking until the topping bubbles, about 5 minutes. Transfer to a cooling rack and cool completely.

GINGERBREAD APPLE PIE

SERVES 8–12

I invented this one day when I couldn't choose between baking an apple pie or gingerbread, and it's been a festive tradition ever since, even if I don't go to a family gathering and it's just my husband, me, and my cats. Truth be told, I hate rolling out pie crust so the crumb topping and pressed crust is a sweet relief for me. As my sister and I say, "This is jood." (We think pronouncing all g's as j's is funny; try it, you'll see.)

For the crust:
175g/6oz plain flour
115g/4oz brown sugar
1 teaspoon ground ginger
1 teaspoon ground cinnamon
1/4 teaspoon ground allspice
1/2 teaspoon salt
1 teaspoon baking powder
115g/4oz non-hydrogenated margarine, softened
1 tablespoon molasses
2 tablespoons cold water

For the filling:
900g/2lb Granny Smith apples (about 8), peeled, cored, and thinly sliced
115g/4oz brown sugar
1 teaspoon ground cinnamon
1/4 teaspoon ground or freshly grated nutmeg
1/4 teaspoon ground allspice
1/2 teaspoon ground ginger
Pinch ground cloves
3 tablespoons pure maple syrup
1 tablespoon rapeseed oil
2 tablespoons tapioca starch or arrowroot

Make the crust:

> Sift together the flour, sugar, spices, salt, and baking powder. Add the margarine one tablespoonful at a time and cut in with a pastry cutter, knife, or your fingertips. Drizzle the molasses and water over the dough, mixing with your fingertips until the crumbs of dough begin to cling together. Set aside 115g/4oz of the dough. Gather together the rest of the dough and knead it into a ball. Press it evenly into the bottom and sides of a pie dish and bake for 10 minutes.

Make the filling:

> While the crust bakes, combine in a mixing bowl all the filling ingredients except the tapioca starch. Sprinkle the tapioca over the apple mixture and mix until the starch is dissolved.

Assemble the pie:

> Fill the pie crust with the apple mixture, and crumble the remaining dough over the filling. Cover with foil and bake for 20 more minutes. Remove the foil and bake 30 minutes more; the filling should be bubbling and the apples should be tender. Serve warm or at room temperature.

⋯⊹ **PUNK POINTS**

> Apple corers can be a pain, so if you hate them or don't have one or both, just cut the apple as close to the core as you can. If you do use one, spray it with oil first to make it easier to get the core out of the corer once it's cored (say that five times fast).

SERVES 8–12

This is a really pretty tart, golden pears studded with burgundy cranberries. It's also low in sugar. Arrange the pear slices all in the same direction for a really professional look. You'll need a 23cm/9in loose bottomed flan tin for this recipe. If you don't have one, you can use a pie plate.

For the crust:
4 tablespoons slivered almonds
115g/4oz plain flour
1/4 teaspoon salt
3 tablespoons cold rice milk
3 tablespoons rapeseed oil

For the filling:
4 pears, peeled, cored, cut in half lengthwise then sliced lengthwise into 5mm/1/4in thick slices
4 tablespoons sugar
2 tablespoons arrowroot
1 tablespoon finely chopped crystallized ginger
4 tablespoons fresh cranberries, sliced in half
1/2 teaspoon almond extract
1 tablespoon water
1 teaspoon ground cinnamon
1/2 teaspoon freshly grated nutmeg

Prepare the crust:

> Heat a small frying pan over medium heat for 2 minutes. Place the slivered almonds in the pan and heat until golden brown, stirring often for 3 to 5 minutes. Transfer to a blender or food processor and pulse the toasted almonds to a fine powder.

> In a large mixing bowl, sift together the flour, ground almonds, and salt. Sprinkle on the rice milk and oil and stir together with a fork. Form the dough into a ball and flatten into a disc. Wrap in clingfilm and refrigerate for half an hour.

> Preheat oven to 190°C/375°F/gas mark 5. Place the chilled dough between two sheets of waxed paper. Roll into a 25cm/10in circle. Peel off the top layer of paper and place the dough paper side up in a flan tin. Remove the top sheet of paper and use your fingers to press the dough into the bottom and sides of the tin. Remove any excess dough so the top edges of the dough are flush with the top of the tin.

For the filling:

> Combine the pears, sugar, arrowroot, crystallized ginger, fresh cranberries, almond extract, water, cinnamon, and nutmeg. Toss gently to combine the ingredients. Layer the pear mixture in the tart shell, evenly distributing the cranberries as you go. If there is some liquid left over, pour it in as well. Cover the pan with foil and bake at 190°C/375°F/gas mark 5 for 30 minutes. Remove the foil and bake 15 minutes more. Remove from oven and let cool before serving.

···❖ **PUNK POINTS**

> To core pears easily, cut in half and use a teaspoon to remove the seeds.

STRAWBERRY SHORTCAKES

SERVES 12

Get a big forkful of the scone soaked in the strawberry sauce with a touch of the Macadamia Crème and it is just, do I say "heavenly" too often? Well, it's heavenly.

Scones (page 48)
Macadamia Crème (recipe follows)

For the strawberry sauce:
900g/2lb strawberries, hulled and sliced
90g/3¹/₂oz sugar
1 tablespoon pure maple syrup
1 teaspoon vanilla extract

> Make the sauce before making the scones and crème because the strawberries need to sit for an hour.

> Place all the sauce ingredients in a bowl, stirring to make sure all the strawberries are coated with sugar. Cover and chill for at least an hour; the strawberries will develop a sauce on their own. That's all there is to making the sauce.

> Split open the scones, spoon in some of the strawberry sauce, cover, and dollop on some Macadamia Crème. Add a few more sliced strawberries to the top, serve.

MACADAMIA CRÈME

Takes five minutes to make, several hours to chill. I use this crème on puddings or on desserts with fruit toppings, including pancakes and waffles. It is easily modified by adding a touch of cinnamon or zest of orange or lemon. It's not fluffy like whipped cream, but it does taste just as good. Try it on Chocolate Pudding (page 238).

60g/2¹/2oz roasted macadamias (see Punk Points)
3 tablespoons soy milk
3 tablespoons icing sugar
¹/2 teaspoon vanilla extract
125ml/4fl oz rapeseed oil

> In a food processor or strong blender, pulverize the roasted macadamias to form a fine powder. Add the soy milk and blend to form a thick paste. Add the icing sugar and vanilla, and blend again. Add the oil in a steady stream while blending. The mixture will resemble a thick liquid. Transfer to a container with a tight lid or a bowl covered in clingfilm, and chill for several hours, preferably overnight.

···⊹ PUNK POINTS

If you can't find roasted macadamias that aren't salted, place raw macadamias on a baking sheet in a 180°C/350°F/gas mark 4 oven for 8 minutes, flipping them after 4 minutes. Or, buy roasted salted ones and rinse the salt off and pat dry.

STRAWBERRY-RHUBARB-PEACH PIE

SERVES 8

Ah, the bounties of summer. This is an obvious pie to make when the farmers' market is overflowing with luscious strawberries, juicy peaches, and tart rhubarb.

Double Pie Crust (recipe follows)
225g/8oz strawberries, sliced 5mm/1/4in thick
2 medium peaches, pitted, peeled, and sliced 1cm/1/2in thick
   (see Punk Points, page 237)
225g/8oz rhubarb stalks, sliced 1cm/1/2in thick
   (discard all leaves; they are poisonous)
75g/3oz sugar
1/4 teaspoon ground cardamom
1/2 teaspoon ground cinnamon
2 tablespoons tapioca starch or arrowroot or cornflour
3 tablespoons maple syrup

> Divide the pie crust dough in slightly unequal halves and roll out each crust into a disc onto parchment paper. The smaller crust should be the diameter of the top of your baking tin; the larger one should be 7.5cm/3in wider to allow for the tin's depth plus a 1cm/1/2in overhang all around. Chill until ready to use.

> Preheat oven to 220°C/425°F/gas mark 7.

> Line a 23cm/9in pie dish with the larger disc of pastry dough, allowing 1cm/1/2in of crust to hang over the edges of the pan.

> Place the fruit and rhubarb in a mixing bowl and add the sugar and spices, mixing to distribute the sugar. Sprinkle in the tapioca starch, mix to incorporate, then add the maple syrup and mix again. Transfer to the pastry-lined pie dish.

> Take the top crust and place it face down on top of the pie; peel back the parchment paper. Fold the overhanging bottom crust back over the edges of the top crust and crimp the pastry together with your thumb and forefinger. Bake for 20 minutes, then reduce the heat to 180°C/350°F/gas mark 4 and bake for 25 to 30 minutes, or until the crust is golden and the juices are bubbling; let cool for a few hours before serving.

SERVES 8

For the filling:
8 peeled and sliced fresh peaches
175g/6oz brown sugar
1 teaspoon ground cinnamon
2 teaspoons vanilla extract
2 tablespoons tapioca starch or arrowroot or cornflour

For the cobbler topping:
115g/4oz plain flour
1$1/2$ teaspoons baking powder
1 teaspoon ground cinnamon
$1/2$ teaspoon ground allspice
3 tablespoons brown sugar, plus extra for sprinkling on crust
3 tablespoons vegetable oil
150ml/$1/4$ pint rice or soy milk
1 teaspoon vanilla extract

> Preheat oven to 230°C/450°F/gas mark 8 and have ready a 23 x 33cm/ 9 x 13in baking dish—preferably Pyrex or ceramic.

Prepare the filling:

> Mix all filling ingredients in the baking dish, set aside.

Prepare the topping:

> In a medium-size mixing bowl, sift together all the dry ingredients; create a well in the centre, add the liquid ingredients, and mix with a wooden spoon until just combined. Drop by tablespoonfuls over the filling, leaving 2.5-5cm/1-2in of peaches between each spoonful. Sprinkle a little extra brown sugar over the top.

> Bake for about 30 minutes, until the filling is bubbling and the top is browned.

···⟩ **PUNK POINTS**

> To peel peaches, blanch them quickly in boiling water for about 45 seconds, then remove with a slotted spoon, cool, and peel. I am all for laziness and the energy you spend blanching will save you a ton of energy trying to peel the peaches without blanching.

CHOCOLATE PUDDING

MAKES 4 SERVINGS

Pudding is the ultimate comfort food for me. This is a fast, yummy, and satisfying treat that you can make with ingredients you probably have on hand. Try the variations below, and top with Macadamia Crème (page 235).

475ml/17fl oz soy milk
3 tablespoons arrowroot or tapioca starch
115g/4oz sugar
5 tablespoons cocoa powder
1 teaspoon vanilla extract
1/8 teaspoon almond extract

> In a small saucepan off the heat whisk together the soy milk and arrowroot until the arrowroot is dissolved. Add the sugar and cocoa powder. Place over medium heat and whisk constantly until the mixture thickens, about 7 minutes. Once the mixture starts to bubble and is quite thick, turn the heat off. Mix in the extracts. Ladle the pudding into four wineglasses or ramekins, and chill in fridge for at least an hour and up to overnight. If you're leaving them in the fridge overnight, don't forget to cover them with clingfilm once they are chilled, to prevent a skin from forming.

···⟩ **VARIATIONS**

> **Chocolate Orange Pudding:** Omit the almond extract; add along with the vanilla 1 1/2 tablespoons of finely grated orange zest (between 1 and
2 oranges) and 1 tablespoon of orange liqueur.

> **Chocolate Coconut Pudding:** Replace 250ml/8fl oz of the soy milk with 250ml/8fl oz of coconut milk, omit the almond extract, and add 1 teaspoon of coconut extract; sprinkle with desiccated coconut after pouring into wineglasses.

> Also, try adding 50g/2oz chopped walnuts or other nuts.

SERVES 4–6

In Mexico, cinnamon is often used to enhance the flavour of chocolate, as if chocolate needs enhancing (but I have to admit that cinnamon and chocolate do taste good together). This creamy dessert is a nice ending to any meal Mexican or otherwise—it's impressive and unexpected while being ridiculously easy. Serve chilled in a wide-mouthed wineglass, or a small bowl, topped with Macadamia Crème (see page 235).

200g/7oz sushi or arborio rice, rinsed
350ml/12fl oz water
475ml/16fl oz soy milk
4 tablespoons cocoa powder
1/4 teaspoon ground cinnamon
50g/2oz plain chocolate
5 tablespoons pure maple syrup
1 teaspoon vanilla extract

> Place the rinsed rice, water, and 350ml/12fl oz of the soy milk in a small saucepan, cover, and bring to a boil. Lower heat and cook at a low simmer for 10 minutes, until the rice is mostly cooked.

> Add the cocoa, cinnamon, and plain chocolate, and stir until well combined and the chocolate is melted. Add the remaining soy milk, and the maple syrup and vanilla. Stir constantly for 5 minutes; if it looks too thick add a little more soy milk.

> Remove from heat and let sit until it is at room temperature, then cover with clingfilm and chill for an hour and serve.

MEXICAN CHOCOLATE RICE PUDDING

INDEX